Into a Room

selected poems of William Soutar

edited and with an introduction by
Carl MacDougall
&
Douglas Gifford

Argyll
publishing

in association with

PERTH &
KINROSS
COUNCIL

© National Library of Scotland
© Introduction
Carl MacDougall
& Douglas Gifford 2000

First published 2000
Argyll Publishing
Glendaruel
Argyll PA22 3AE
www.deliberatelythirsty.com
in association with
Perth & Kinross Council
AK Bell Library
York Place
Perth PH2 6PN

The authors have asserted their
moral rights.

**British Library Cataloguing-in-
Publication Data.
A catalogue record for this
book is available from the
British Library.**

ISBN 1 902831 22 5

Subsidised by the Scottish Arts
Council

Origination
Cordfall Ltd, Glasgow

Printing
ColourBooks Ltd, Dublin

Contents

Acknowledgements

IN HIS introduction to the *Poems of William Soutar: a new selection* W.R.Aitken writes that Soutar's judgement on his Whigmaleeries – that they 'ought to make rather amusing and unusual reading and add a little to the Scots tradition' – is modestly apt. 'His contribution,' he adds, 'to the wealth of Scottish literature is substantially and undeservedly neglected.' This view has been the impetus for this selection.

Anyone who now approaches Soutar's poetry must be aware of William Aitken's huge contribution to Soutar scholarship and we are pleased to acknowledge our debt and to record our admiration. Similarly it would be ungracious not to acknowledge the debt Soutar scholars owe Alexander Scott. His critical biography *Still Life* and selection from the Soutar journals, published as *Diaries of a Dying Man,* are landmarks.

While its true worth may not have been recognised, Soutar's work has scarcely been neglected. The Scottish Music Archive currently holds more that a hundred settings of Soutar poems by composers such as Francis George Scott, Ronald Stevenson, Bill Sweeney, Martin Dalby and James Macmillan. Macmillan falls between two stools – his arrangement of 'The Tryst' for female voice, two clarinets, viola, cello and double bass makes an interesting comparison to his singing the tune he put to the words with the Whistlebinkies folk group. Folk singers who have set Soutar's texts include Sheila Douglas, Dave Whyte and the Sangsters. This latter group have given Soutar a new audience, for along with poems by Helen B. Cruickshank and Violet Jacob, singers effortlessly pass Soutar's writing onto a new audience who now know these poems only as songs.

A play based on Soutar's life *Gang Doon Wi a Sang* by Joy

Hendry, as well as her radio play on Soutar, Tom Fleming's one-man show *The Quiet Room* and successive William Soutar Writing Fellows based at his former home in Perth have injected fresh interest in his work. The contributions of the former Writing Fellows Raymond Vettese, Donald Campbell, John Herdman and Robert Alan Jamieson deserve special mention. We gratefully acknowledge permission to quote from John Herdman's essay 'The Challenge of Limitation'.

In thanking the National Library of Scotland for permission to use the poems, the Scottish Arts Council and Perth and Kinross Council Library Services, special mention must be given to Mike Moir for his continuous generous support and friendship and to Dawn Morrison who keyed in the text.

We would like to thank Johnny Rodger and Tim Green for the material on ankylosing spondylitis and to record the generous help of the Soutar family, especially the late Mollie Mackenzie and family and Willie's cousin, Jamie Soutar. We are also grateful to the surviving members of the MacQueen family, especially to Eleanor Bain, for allowing us to use valuable family material.

Carl MacDougall
Douglas Gifford
September 2000

Introduction

I

WILLIAM SOUTAR (1898–1943) is one of the greatest poets Scotland has produced and one of our finest diarists. In his journals, hopes for his poetry and some first ideas sit alongside philosophical and social discussions. Ezra Pound told him to drag himself into the twentieth century, not to use a dead language. Yet MacDiarmid considered his work a sufficient threat to omit sizeable sections from the *Collected Poems* Soutar's father and MacDiarmid's benefactor had commissioned him to edit.

MacDiarmid's introductory essay to the *Collected Poems* is scarcely flattering. At a time when MacDiarmid's pronouncements on Scottish literature went virtually unchallenged, certainly in public, Soutar was depicted as a minor poet. While it is true that MacDiarmid sought to portray all contemporary and near contemporary poets as minor compared to himself, Soutar's case is somewhat different. He is cast as a heroic soul whose illness had a debilitating, even a deleterious effect on his work, an image which has remained. MacDiarmid did Soutar and himself a disservice and the time has come for a reassessment. MacDiarmid's place in Scottish literature is secure. Soutar deserves a fresh interpretation and evaluation.

Nor is he alone in this requirement. 'Despite the excellence of the poetry that was being written, the justifications surrounding it could give the impression that a romantically inferiorist insularity was preferred. It was the failure of criticism, a flaw in the literary atmosphere, and it helped to make Scottish poetry as a whole look like a subject best left to its participants and native readers to squabble over,' writes Douglas Dunn in 'Language and Liberty', his Introduction to *The Faber Book of Twentieth Century Scottish Poetry*, adding:

> 'One consequence of that state of affairs was the postponement of criticism in favour of puffery that supports a 'reputation', or the malice, or silence, that destroys or prevents it. Only in recent years have MacLean, MacCaig, Edwin Morgan and W.S. Graham been written about intelligently or at any length, while proper studies of Soutar, Goodsir Smith and Garioch do not exist.'

The thrust of Dunn's point is as relevant as ever.

II

William Soutar was born at 4 South Inch Terrace, Perth, on Thursday 28 April 1898, the only son of John and Margaret Soutar. His father was born in Caputh in 1871, the fourth son of a farmer, and was apprenticed to a joiner at fourteen. He moved to Perth in 1895. Margaret Smith was a native of Perth, daughter of a police sergeant and youngest of a family of three. The couple were engaged in 1896 and married on 10 June 1897. Not long after the wedding, John Soutar and a friend, Tom McQueen, formed the joinery contracting business of Soutar & McQueen.

The Soutars were Scots in speech and religion, members of the United Original Secession Church, the Auld Lichts, whose strict observances were impressed upon their son. 'The religious element has coloured all my life,' he wrote. 'Brought up in a home which still retained the services of grace and family worship – the Scottish Sabbath echoed for me all thr' the week.'

Soutar attended Perth's Southern District School from 1903 to 1912. He described himself as 'a terrible nuisance and was strapped practically every day, actually isolated from the class, for a time, to a desk out on the floor.'

In 1911 he and another pupil, James Armstrong, led a strike. 'We had learned that the miners were on strike somewhere, and from emulation rather than conscious sympathy decided to act likewise when the interval bell should ring.' About forty pupils marched across the South Inch singing and shouting. More than half deserted. When the interval was over, Soutar and Armstrong formed the others two deep and marched back to school, where they were met by a teacher who told them 'the strikers would be struck.'

He was a pupil at Perth Academy until 1916. 'Then I was one of the fleetest . . . one of the strongest: first in my year at most things: I was writing poetry: I was in love: I was popular both in the classroom and on the playing field: I never reached this condition of living fullness again except in brief moments.'

Shooting results from the Christmas 1914 issue of *Perth Academy Magazine* show him to be a proficient shot. His first published poem 'The Academy Boy' appeared in the magazine's Midsummer 1915 issue, another poem, entitled 'War' appeared at Midsummer 1916 and the Christmas 1916 issue shows he was the school's high jump champion.

Later in his Common-Day Book he recalled, 'Moments of exhilaration – My earliest recollection . . . takes me back to a summer day when I may have been seven or eight years old. I was leaping along the Shore Road, near the old sawmill, with the dust inches deep under my bare feet. Every now and then I would spring straight up into the air and bring my feet together down-pointed like a ballet-dancer – then for one ecstatic second I was certain that I hovered.'

He had been writing poetry since schooldays, and though he initially intended to study medicine at Edinburgh University, he transferred to the arts faculty after a year. In July 1922, Soutar sent a selection of his poems to C.M.Grieve, who was then editing *Scottish Chapbook*. In accepting three poems, MacDiarmid said he would be 'greatly disappointed if splendid work does not come from your pen.'

In November 1922, Soutar's first collection of poetry was

accepted by Alexander Gardner of Paisley. The cost was met by Soutar's father and *Gleanings by an Undergraduate* appeared anonymously in February, 1923. 'Soutar the poet,' his father wrote after costing his son's first collection, 'son of Soutar the joiner . . . I like it fine.'

The Soutars were an intensely close and loving family. While he was away from home, in the Navy, at university or convalescing in the Orkney Isles, Willie wrote to his parents every week, and they wrote to him, often silly, scribbled notes of little significance to anyone but themselves, teasing each other, making family jokes. The result presents a unique family portrait.

John Soutar emerges as a man full of practicality. He continually offers advice and complains about having to deal with bits of paper, saying he is easier in dealing with hard facts than ideas. When Willie's coat was stolen, his father sent money by return, enclosing warmest wishes to his son and 'a hard kick in the arse' to the bugger who stole the coat. He thinks the poems his son published in *The Student* were 'beautiful'.

Margaret Soutar wrote poetry, mostly of a religious nature, but she was certainly capable of discussing what she read on comparative terms with her son. She asks his advice and opinion, specifically mentioning favourite writers such as John Ruskin and Charles Lamb. She kept a notebook of favourite verses and a book of reading notes, dedicated 'To my beloved boy.' She wrote prayers and discussed Milton's 'On His Blindness' and Alfred Noyes' 'Creation' – which 'Dad thought was rubbish' – in letters to her son. She mentions birds at the window, constructs a game of make-believe for tired mothers and warns her son to be careful of certain women.

'Dad,' she says, 'is always so giving.' On their fiftieth wedding anniversary John Soutar enclosed a letter with his gift, signing himself 'your lover'. On the first anniversary of Willie's death, she wrote a celebratory poem for her son, and his name appears on the manuscript or margins of a number of her other verses:

Men who have known him – other men
Will ever his memory keep:
And though the sower is taken,
We the harvest will reap.

He kept their letters and they kept his. Margaret Soutar put Willie's poems into the church magazine where some of her own work appeared.

Following his enlistment in the Royal Navy in 1916, William Soutar completed his basic training on HMS *Eclipse*, crossed the Atlantic on HMS *Carnarvon* and witnessed the surrender of the German fleet, while serving on HMS *Colossus*. Towards the end of his service on *Colossus* he contracted food poisoning which is said to have led to his disability. Returning from leave on December 8, 1918, he wrote to his parents complaining, 'For goodness sake laugh. I haven't to move a finger's length without the aid of a crutch.'

He failed to respond to treatment and was sent to the Royal Naval Hospital, Granton, Edinburgh, on December 23, was transferred to the Royal Naval Hospital at Larbert on December 31, where the chief surgeon recommended him for leave until demobilisation.

On 22 October 1923, Soutar began the first in a series of consultations with Professor (later Sir) John Fraser. The massage treatment began in November, the following month Soutar had his first injection and his treatment continued for seven years.

On 23 May 1924, the Soutars moved into their new house, which Willie christened Inglelowe; a semi-detached villa Soutar's father and his business partner Tom McQueen had built to their own specifications. The McQueens occupied the other half of the building. Inglelowe is not the ten-roomed mansion described by Alexander Scott in *Still Life*. It is a perfectly respectable bungalow, typical of the period. And surely Robert Alan Jamieson is also correct in suggesting it was built as a calling card for Soutar & McQueen.

Although initially able to get about and do odd jobs in the

house and garden, Soutar was unfitted for any strenuous activity; even party games were denied him, though he took up the fiddle and learned to play the banjo-mandoline and tin whistle.

His health continued to deteriorate. In 1929 he contracted pneumonia and pleurisy and the decline in his physical condition was permanent. Despite successive attempts at treatment, lengthy spells in hospital and extensive periods of convalescence, his condition, now diagnosed as ankylosing spondylitis, worsened and in June 1930, following an unsuccessful operation, Soutar was confined to bed, where he remained for the rest of his life.

The dining room became his bedroom, a downstairs room opposite the bathroom at the centre of the house, with an outlook into the back garden, Craigie Hill and the sky. The outlook was photographed by his friend Alex Galloway and the only known photograph of William Soutar in bed was taken by Helen Cruickshank, standing on a chair at the door of Willie's room with a single exposure in her camera. Soutar always dressed in a freshly laundered shirt, bow tie and sometimes wore a jacket, '. . . to prove, of course, that only my lower limbs are asleep.'

Soutar received what was considered to be the best medical attention available at the time. It has been generally accepted that food poisoning led to Soutar's debility. Perhaps this notion was fostered by Sir John Fraser, but a booklet on ankylosing spondylitis published by the Arthritis Research Campaign says the disease has no known cause, nor is there a cure. Medicine can only relieve symptoms, improve spinal mobility and allow the patient to lead a normal life. It and the *AS News* (The Journal of the National Ankylosing Spondylitis Society) underline certain features of the illness. 'AS takes a different course in different people, and no two cases are exactly the same,' it says, warning that not everyone will return to normal. Rest is recommended, but confinement in bed 'can hasten the stiffening of the spine.' Lying flat on one's front for twenty minutes twice a day, deep breathing and correct posture are recommended. Regular, daily exercise is important and swimming is the best, but a small exercise routine is illustrated.

Soutar's journals brim with details of his illness and treatments, with continual admiration for John Fraser, until he was eventually confined to bed. From then, until his final decline, the entries take on a note of recall. Smells are especially important and individual memories are usually placed in a significant context.

'There are moments in every life when the life within us seems to decide,' he wrote on Wednesday, 5 June 1935. 'Thus it spoke to me, after I had learned the nature of my trouble, when suddenly I halted in the dusk beside the pillars of West St George's, Edinburgh, and stood for a moment bareheaded saying over to myself, 'Now I can be a poet.'

Illness, Soutar said, forced him 'to stare upon a corner of reality.' It no more made him a poet any more than Byron's limp or Auden's stammer aided their creativity; but Soutar had difficulty finding his voice and illness allowed him to turn his energies to poetry, a career he had long since decided to follow.

His famous phrase, written in July 1931, that he did not mind being ill, because he was too well looked after, appears to be based on truth. This feeling seems to have settled in Soutar's second year of confinement, when he becomes perfectly pleased with his own company.

'How pleasant to know one has a couple of hours to oneself,' he wrote in May 1932. 'How subtle is my form of self-flattery. What I am tacitly saying all the time to so many of my friends, "When you leave me I shall be in much better company." '

Earlier he complained of being assailed by 'drably respectable minds'. And by July was asserting himself as 'truly a fellow who does not desire to be surrounded with people. I suppose that Finlayson is the only friend I would welcome as a regular weekly visitor.' James Finlayson had been Soutar's friend from childhood. He painted Soutar's portrait when they were students in Edinburgh and drew Soutar in bed, complete with bow tie and jacket, as well as a sensitive recumbent pose.

He also drew Soutar's personal symbol of the unicorn.

Soutar's only other needs were beyond him. He often wished he were able to walk about, choose his own company, occasionally leap and dance, see a Chaplin film or walk over Callerfountain. 'Living in so comfortable a cell as my own leaves little cause for complaint – yet to bring the world picture into it I should have a second window from which I could look out on the sea: and near enough also for me to hear it.'

Despite his complaints, Soutar was a sociable body. Five hundred and seventy five people came in 1937, 680 in 1938, 769 in 1939, 713 in 1940 and 623 in the last year of his life. Wilson Street became a centre for the Scottish Renaissance. His address book shows the range of his contacts and his diaries show that, with the exception of Lewis Grassic Gibbon, every major figure of the Scottish Renaissance not only came to visit him, but was on agreeable personal terms. He and Gibbon appear not to have been in touch, though they certainly knew and admired each other's work. After Gibbon's death Soutar chides himself for the coldness of his response to the loss. 'Have we, in the words of Lawrence, not the "courage of our tenderness": are we too afraid of giving our self away?'

III

That illness concentrated Soutar's energies and made his achievements possible is beyond doubt. Yet the fact that he was almost certainly in constant pain, that he had to bring the world to him and simultaneously pass his days gave him certain obsessions. He was a dedicated keeper of personal trivia, recording, for example, what letters arrived, who sent them, and when he replied. He read *Encyclopaedia Britannica, Chambers' Twentieth Century Dictionary* and Jamieson's *Dictionary of the Scottish Language*, ticking words he memorised, or items of interest.

Soutar recorded his earnings and the poems he read, his gramophone records and books, as well as the stories, jokes and anecdotes he heard, items he would later use as a springboard into poetry. He contributed Perthshire words and phrases to the Scottish National Dictionary and kept Scots Vocabulary Notebooks, where words were shown in the context of a sentence, as well as diaries, journals and dream books, where items were recorded as notes for his poems. The earliest drafts of many poems are the hand-written copies which would be typed up by a typist at Soutar & McQueen. While he appears to have worked and reworked many ideas, he obviously depended heavily on the original thought, many poems arriving in his notebooks complete.

In his Introduction to the *Collected Poems* MacDiarmid comments on Soutar's powers of observation: '. . . not a leaf stirred, no bird or insect moved, no colour of sky or flower changed hue or tone without his noticing it and describing it in his diary.'

But observation is often just the beginning. Soutar's profound humanity soon takes over, making striking and surprising comparisons, almost always leading us to a place which is not at all obvious in the beginning. Some of these pieces stand comparison with the best lyrics being written at the time, often mirroring MacDiarmid's in their profundity and surprising conclusions.

> Lift up your e'en and greet nae mair,
> The black trees on the brae are still;
> And lichtsome, in the mirkl'd air,
> A star gangs gladly owre the hill.
>
> Sae far awa fae worldly soun'
> In laneliness it glimmers by;
> And the cauld licht comes kindly doun
> On earth and a' her misery.

As with Burns and MacDiarmid before him, Soutar seems to control both image and observation, releasing the information in a way that seems natural rather than crafted.

His poems are full of such moments, where the physical world he sees beyond the room combines with a positive acceptance of his place, rather than his fate. Some moments, particularly in the Diaries, carry the suggestion of how he would want to be, rather than the way he is, and though his incapacity still attracts the casual observer, it is hardly in a voyeuristic sense, but rather as a means of entry. It provides an approach to the work in the way that personal details of a writer's life often lend or enhance interest. With Soutar it has almost worked in reverse; that because he was ill, there is little more to be found.

His illness gives a shattering poignancy to a poem like 'The Tryst'. It is a remarkable affirmation of life in the face of illness and incapacity, bringing separate strands of his life together, his dreams together with his personal circumstances. Like most of Soutar's work, it could equally have been written by an able-bodied man; but the fact that Soutar was not able-bodied gives the poem a piquancy it would otherwise lose.

The theme is well-known to folklorists; a number of Night Visiting Songs exist in the Scottish folk tradition. The theme of a ghostly visitor reconnecting with a former lover is known throughout Europe and is the substance of many ballads and is most obviously found in Scotland in songs such as, 'I'm a Rover', where the lover endures inclement weather and vast distances to be with his love.

Soutar's achievement is to cut through the details making the lyric both personal and universal, using the first line as an echo of loss in the final verse. It is a remarkable piece, using the language of the ballad in such a scaldingly spare way that the poignancy lies not in what is said, dreamed or even remembered, but in the unstated loss and anxieties.

'The Tryst' was first published in *The Spectator*, on 28 May 1932. They paid the poet one pound ten shillings. It is interesting to consider if today's *Spectator* would publish a poem in Scots?

The same poetic interpretation of what he saw extended into a broader, compressed image or extended metaphor is in the diaries. On 29 June 1932 – the day after he wrote, 'It is not a self-compliment to surmise that one had to sacrifice one's body to make a self' – Soutar notes in his diary, 'Just now as I lifted my eyes to the hillside I saw the trees waving like a wall of fire. If only one could respond to life as the earth to the sun – but the heart is so often a trim little garden with neither the luxuriance nor the conflict of the jungle. It is so easy to retreat within the safe walls of mediocrity.'

But something less obvious, and therefore more easily overlooked, is his celebration of the ordinary, the obvious things which surround him, his love of the domestic. Its most unmistakable manifestation is in his humour, but it's part of the impetus behind the poems he wrote for Evelyn, the niece of his mother's cousin whose parents were killed in a sailing accident. She joined the family from Australia in 1927. He often found his inspiration in conversation. Small anecdotes, even stories, become poems. The Bairnsangs and the Whigmaleeries can be seen as his celebration of the ordinary.

On 28 August 1932, he wrote, 'My life's purpose is to write poetry – but behind the poetry must be the vision of a fresh revelation for men.' Art, he said, is for all and the greatest art proves it.

'To this end,' writes John Herdman, 'he sought an art which should 'grow out of the experience of humble folk and their daily toil: in short parables after the fashion of the gospel.' (28 January 1933) A little later, however, he indicates that this should not centre only on 'rural lyricism' and that a 'flight from industrialism' such as he observed in much contemporary verse in the Scots vernacular must be seen as a 'cowardly retreat.' (18 October 1934) This is a recurrent note in the diaries through the years: that 'the individual gift can grow to fullness only when it is nourished by a magnanimity learned from communality.' (16 May 1937) There is no doubt that this reiteration springs at least in part from Soutar's worries about the effects of his necessary solitariness upon his attitude towards his art, worries which encouraged him to make the most of the opportunities for social contact which were open to him, to learn to see the best in people and to develop his natural gift for friendship.

It also seems certain that Soutar's quest for spiritual development forced him to abandon the strictures of the church in which he was raised and to find a personal faith where his socialist and nationalist beliefs contributed to his spiritual development. His involvement with the pacifist movements of the 1930s and his regular correspondence with John Middleton Murry testify to his acceptance of Christian Socialist ideals.

Murry was an influential figure. He was Katherine Mansfield's husband and D.H.Lawrence's publisher, and Soutar was an avowed Lawrentian. Many of Soutar's poems were published in the *Adelphi* magazine, which Murry edited and where John Duncan Ferguson was art editor. 'Murry's is the one contemporary mind – apart from D.H.Lawrence's – whose "identity" . . . has "pressed itself" upon me,' Soutar wrote on 27 March 1938, praising Murry's study of Keats and Shakespeare as a critical masterpiece. 'This has continued now for about a dozen or more years – and seems likely to continue until the end. In Murry I see a spiritual growth. . .'

And it was Soutar's quest for spiritual growth which allowed him to respond to what he saw as the generosity of life. 'His whole attitude to life,' wrote Alexander Scott in his Introduction to *Diaries of a Dying Man*, ' – kindliness in personal relationships, concern for others, emotional and intellectual honesty – was rooted in the religion in which he was born and bred.' He urged acceptance of life on life's terms, no matter the fate.

On 10 January 1933, in the third year of his confinement, he wrote,

> 'For some time past I have been growing towards a
> realisation of the generosity of life – and that it is this
> lively generousness which is exemplified in great men and
> women: the seal which distinguishes them. No finer
> symbol of this has come my way than that of Isadora
> Duncan dancing with breasts so full of milk that they

overflowed – the rich, natural freedom of this woman's life, its very waywardness, is like a flower in the waste land of the machines. . . What is love but that generous recep- tiveness and recreation mentioned above.

'When I know this grace than I shall give back to life something of that richness which life has given to me. I can but blame some fatal flaw in my self's self for the humiliation of a fine body.'

The idea of personal responsibility is central to Soutar's thinking. And though he moves from the notion, however tacitly stated, that the worm may be in the bud, by Wednesday, 20 November 1935, he seems to have found a self which allows his mind and spirit to develop and grow while his body atrophies, suggesting he believes the life within us is more than personal, and we find this by personal examination.

'Our own life would make us wise if we were but willing to stand away from our self for a moment and look upon our history in detachment. What may such a glimpse teach myself? Surely that the spirit of man is stronger than his chains. From a world I entered a university, from a quadrangle I came into a garden, from a garden into a house, from a room into a bed – only a coffin can complete the "cellular series". Yet . . . my mind has continued to grow and if growth is not maintained the thwarting element will be in myself. I should have no doubt functioned differently if the world had remained there from which to choose – but the potential (core of self) cannot be smothered by environment.'

This progression became his poem 'Autobiography', written as a diary entry in July, 1937. And as death approaches, life becomes more of a gift and the gift itself becomes more precious.

IV

W.R.Aitken first recognised Soutar's central duality of the symbols of Unicorn and Gowk in poetry. The following is based on that insight, together with an attempt to refute MacDiarmid's limiting assessments of Soutar's work in his 1948 introduction to the *Collected Poems*. These assessments are typical of MacDiarmid's evaluation of the achievements of previous and contemporary Scottish writers – typically he reduces others in a manner which simultaneously endorses MacDiarmid's claim that Scottish literature was in the doldrums, the Cinderella event of European culture, before he came on the Scottish scene, and his implicit claim that he, MacDiarmid, was the unrivalled leader, the *Narodbogonoset*, of the Scottish Renaissance.

This is not the place to challenge the view that the modern Scottish Renaissance began with MacDiarmid, except to suggest that it is hardly a culturally barren country which produces in the period 1880-1920 novelists like Stevenson, Alexander, Oliphant, MacDonald, Douglas Brown, Munro, Barrie, S.R. Crockett, the Findlater sisters, MacDougall Hay and Catherine Carswell; poets like James Thomson, James Young Geddes (arguably the greatest radical poet between Burns and MacDiarmid), John Davidson, Marion Angus and Violet Jacob.

Till the end of his life Soutar agonised about his country's identity and mindset in ways that often resulted in ironic and sometimes embittered poetry, scathing in its view of politicians and the so-called Scottish Renaissance. We believe he should not be seen in the shadow of MacDiarmid, an unquestioning disciple in his leader's self-centred movement. Soutar has his own personal renaissance, which is not to be limited by an assessment which sees him preoccupied with bringing the Doric back to Scotland on a cock-horse. MacDiarmid's view limits Soutar, seeing a talented but unfortunately restricted poet writing below his full potential, either in escapist fantasy, or in rhymes for children, producing in *Seeds in the Wind* (1933) what MacDiarmid regarded as 'a minor classic'. Soutar's own classifications of his poetry have perhaps given readers a false sense of a qualitative hierarchy within his achievement; the impression which can wrongly be taken from his generic titles for groupings of poems, Bairnrhymes and Whigmaleeries, is that of diversion, amusement, and withdrawal from MacDiarmid's 'Scotland now', with its agenda for breaking with a supposedly suffocating past and for radical national social and intellectual change.

If Soutar is removed from MacDiarmid's shadow, and instead placed in the context of all Scottish poetry, and seen as the inheritor of traditions from Dunbar and Henryson, the Ballads, Ramsay and Fergusson, Hogg, Stevenson, Davidson, Angus and Jacob, then he can be perceived as a unique representative of the entire tradition. Soutar became its celebrant to create a personal renaissance for a dying man, a renaissance within which he could find new identity, joining, with the underlying, timeless voices of the poets he celebrates in 'The Auld Tree', his most ambitious and explicit homage to his fellows.

There is no doubt, of course, that MacDiarmid was amongst these poets; Soutar dedicated this poem to him, and the inspiration of MacDiarmid's early lyrics is everywhere in Soutar's work and especially towards the end – but equally we should recognise that he has much in common with, and probably drew extensively from, Edwin Muir's reflective humanity, synthesizing the atavistic vitality of the one with the contemplative tranquillity of the other. He is not a foot soldier in MacDiarmid's debatable movement of Scottish Renaissance, but a makar who resolves his personal tragedy in identification with the human predicament as seen through the entire tradition of Scottish poetry.

With such a relocation, Soutar's truly eclectic, traditionally inspired, but finally unique contribution to Scottish poetry can be recognised. Far more effectively than MacDiarmid, Soutar went, not just 'back to Dunbar', but back to Henryson and the Makars and the Ballads; and if we still allow some weight to T.S.Eliot's notion of individual talent fulfilling itself by working creatively with tradition, then Soutar more than any other

Scottish poet successfully demonstrates how layers of tradition from over five hundred years could be synthesized into an often atemporal beauty, poetry which cannot simply be placed under the banner of 'Scottish Renaissance'.

For Soutar all Scottish poetry was alive; poems like 'The Tryst', 'Birthday', 'The Whale', 'The Auld Tree', show just how many Scottish poets – including MacDiarmid – were living tradition to him. We suggest that to appreciate Soutar's finest poetry we must follow him as he dreams in the terribly solitary place of his private, sensitive, infinitely courageous mind. He read about the changing Scotland outside his room, and listened with immense patience and kindliness – but with part of his mind ironically aware of his predicament – to his well-meaning but often very boring visitors. But after they left, and after the continual devotion of parents, he must have been sometimes the loneliest man in Scotland. What refuge, what release for a mind in love with the physical world outside, and a body still alive to desire and fulfilment?

Release and fulfilment lay, of course, in the diaries, the letters, and outstandingly, in the poetry. But it is deceptive and unusual poetry, its statement most often made in the short lyric, and the very abundance of these lyrics with their apparent and effortless simplicity tempting the reader to move too quickly over the surface, missing their wry, humane, and often very subtle nuances. The poetry's greatest achievement lies in its transcendence of time and place, so that they part company with here and now, in ways often comparable with the work of Edwin Muir and his disciple Mackay Brown, so that at best its representation of nature, of events, and of human agents, take on a detached unearthliness, and a unplaceable temporality, shot through with observing humour, and expressed in forms and voices drawn from what Soutar hears in his room as the living voices, from past and present, of Scottish poetry – and, in later years, the voices, in rhythm and anecdote, of his ain toun and locality.

Above all, escape lay in the deeply imagined and felt world

of the great supernatural Ballads, in the mirk, twilight, and glamourie where traditionally this world and the Other Landscape meet, where – as Soutar recurrently describes it – his dreams and visions' saftly 'smool awa', 'smool' being his motif-word for the disintegration of dreams and dream-visitors in daylight. And always these shadows and visions reassemble to live again in new dreams and new poems. It is not escapism; rather it is a deeply human paradox which Soutar articulates, that in which desire for the ideal, the vision, co-exists with recognition of earthly limitation and loss. No other poet, with the exception of the Muir of 'The Horses' or 'The Labyrinth' or 'One Foot in Eden', can express the rise and fall of yearning dream and sad realism so well.

Soutar's predicament placed him between MacDiarmid and Gibbon. He shared something of their response to personal tragedy; but, suspended between death and recreation of the self, he was forced in the 1930s to work between oppositions which were his imprisonment, but also the ground of his spiritual escape. These oppositions are on one hand the world of dream, nightmare, false echoes and disillusion, the cheating world of the Gowk, the delusive cuckoo; and on the other the world of vision and commitment to the pursuit of a Keatsian ideal beauty, or an ideal cause such as Scottish Renaissance, often symbolised by the elusive Unicorn.

A host of subordinate tensions and oppositions underlie this primary split between negation and withdrawal, but this dualism dominates. There is on one hand the turning of mind and spirit to the wall; on the other, a willed courage to fight on, together with a visionary assertion of Scottish Renaissance. This tension was resolved only in the last years, with Soutar's recognition that neither side held truth for him. Instead, he turned to his community and his ordinary fellow-Scots, and a sense of immediate place and people for conviction and consolation, with dreams and visions giving way to acceptance of a more mundane, yet richly varied world.

The early 1930s and the debate between delusive dream

and affirmative vision did, however, produce some of his greatest poetry. And these years of fundamental dualism of response to his predicament must not be seen as simplistically viewing the one side of response as bad, and the other as good. Two major qualifications must be made. Firstly, much of the greatest of Soutar's poetry stems from the creative interplay of negation and affirmation, such as 'The Tryst', or the Gowk poems themselves. Secondly, between 1930 and 1943, and underneath the poems of polarisation, Soutar worked successfully with his adaptation of Keats's notion of 'negative capability' to forge an undogmatic humanism which saw his own predicament only too clearly, but increasingly accepted it, expressing acceptance in an immense number of local, apparently unambitious, but in fact deceptively simple poems which celebrate Soutar's kinship with his countrymen and his country.

These final poems of acceptance were hard earned. In 1930 Soutar had a grim prospect. However much parents and friends tried to make it more acceptable, with the ever-darkening awareness of his condition, the view from his room was nevertheless a framed and limited view of changing season and natural event, and with most human events permanently outside. Most of all, he was facing a drastic re-assessment of himself and his personal and creative ambitions. Soutar had been writing poetry mainly in English and for long before this. Indeed, since *Gleanings of an Undergraduate* in 1923, with its Metaphysical-Romantic, rebellious and English-traditional inspiration, a voice which was to continue through *Conflict* in 1931, and to modify into a reflective, calm abhorrence of violence and inequity. This voice was akin to that of Muir in later volumes like *The Solitary Way* (1936), *A Handful of Earth* (1936), and *In the Time of Tyrants* (1939).

It is tempting to simplify Soutar's re-assessment of himself at this point as resulting in a fundamental decision to let 'English' poetry give way to Scots, but such a view would indeed be simplistic. He continued to write in English till he died – although it is true that Soutar's most ambitious English poetry, in *But The Earth Abideth* (1943), was badly received by critics. There is clearly an issue to consider in Soutar's 'two voices', an issue dealt with by Alexander Scott by separating his consideration of poetic achievement into that of 'poet' (poetry in English) and 'makar' (poetry in Scots) – but Soutar uses both languages to serve his search for selfhood and its articulation. It's fair to say that Scots gave Soutar a concision, a dry and traditional irony, and a grotesquerie, which he could not find in English; but by the end both voices were coming from different perspectives to the same view. Re-assessment brought the English Literature-trained poet who initially scorned MacDiarmid and ideas of Scottish Renaissance together with the makar who discovered the Ballads, Henryson, and the Scottish tradition.

The poetry begins its greatest statements with its recognition of limitation. Here is 'The Room'. It is at first a place of confinement; but it becomes a place of rebirth, where Soutar recreates himself, finding in Scottish tradition and poetry a new, more richly humane creative self. The final and moving impression from Soutar's poetry is that of a personal renaissance, whereby Soutar recreates himself in and is recreated by Lowland Scottish tradition and culture. But the war of 'The Room' was fought over more than a decade – and often, the most personal and vivid accounts of confinement and solitude are tersely expressed in his English poetry. 'Cosmos' is the most succinct statement; 'there is a universe within this room', Soutar tells us – but it is a negative space, with its images of monotony and 'the ticking tongue of time' stuttering in silence and dust, marking descent 'from gloom to gloom'. And poem after poem of this period reiterates the 1930s discovery of loneliness.

The reader can easily put together a grouping of poems which would suggest that for several years after 1930 Soutar was bleakly embittered. 'Black Laughter' chillingly recalls Muir's ending to 'The Labyrinth'; dreaming that he has Godly power to help his 'own land'. Soutar awakes, shuddering, hearing insistent, mocking laughter, while 'Beyond Loveliness', opening with a dream of contentment on a hill in the noon-day sun, 'and I at one, within this solitude', closes with the dream broken by the intrusion of the old man with his burden, with 'no eye for nature'; 'with him my thought went down', Soutar concludes, since a dreary death awaits them both. This world seems a cheating dream and, significantly, in an anticipation of his later and most powerful symbolism – 'The Mood' likens the cuckoo's cry in the neighbouring wood to a delusive, tantalising, and unattainable dream, ending with the poet's by now familiar reminder to himself that he must recognise his, and humanity's, final solitude.

'Autobiography', as late as 1937, shows that these dark moods persisted for long, and seems to sum up this confessional bleakness in a spiritual palindrome, its movement forward mockingly echoed in reverse, as it sets womb/ bed/ room/ garden/ town/ country/ earth/ people against people/ earth/ country/ town/ garden/ room/ bed/ womb – an echo to find its image in the delusive Gowk/Cuckoo of future poems.

Understandably however, constant mood swings assert completely opposite views of 'The Room'. 'Reverie' of 1933 seems to echo the sense of a shrinking world, Soutar's room-garden seen as a world 'shrunk into a little garth/and life to phantasy' – but it is precisely in the translation to 'phantasy' that hope arises – in the greener grass and bluer sky of dream, which paradoxically suggests that the world of actual life may be less important and satisfying than that of the dream world. These English poems of the early 1930s could express a strikingly different mood from that of bleak pessimism, as in 'The Return of the Swallow', which is placed against 'the singing sigh' of the cuckoo mood, and startles the blood with 'a quick pulse of joy', akin to the God-like epiphany of 'A Summer Morning' and 'At Peace', which tells us that frequently Soutar was content 'to cease/from mortal busyness and stare/Silent, alone, at peace'.

Already certain images and ideas are clarifying themselves, becoming symbols mocking echo and delusive or affirmative dream; outstandingly, the image and the idea of the Gowk and the Unicorn. They are by no means Soutar's only effective symbols which repudiates entirely MacDiarmid's complaint that Soutar suffered from a serious inability 'to take the mad leap into the symbol'. There is throughout Soutar's work a constant patterning of profound symbols. And in the recurrent allegorical significances Soutar gives to tree, bird, seeds, roots, worm, the brig, the wall, the stone and the graveyard (not to mention lion and whale) there is a richness, which grows with the reader's awareness and familiarity. Gowk-cuckoo and Unicorn-stag stand at the head of this rich motif-patterning. The symbolic significance of these elemental images stands comparison with MacDiarmid's own exploitation of serpent, moon, thistle and the like in poems such as 'A Drunk Man Looks at the Thistle' – although closer analysis shows that where MacDiarmid's symbols are constantly in flux, protean in their significations, representing the play of his imagination and thought, Soutar's are comparatively stable, linked to his positive and negative feelings, and changing mainly as his moods change.

V

Looking at the poetry as a whole, the deepest tension within William Soutar concerned the nature of selfhood. The English poems, around 1930, obsessively asserted the idea of self, or its loss; but paradoxically, about the same time Soutar began the movement towards his greatest triumph, a much more significant personal renaissance or rebirth. It wasn't just for adopted Evelyn or for the children of Scotland that Soutar argued for the return of the Doric on a cock-horse – it was just as much for himself, as he had to recreate part of himself – the deepest creative part – within a Scottish tradition he had ignored or even scorned while an undergraduate.

Yes, he had read Henryson when he should have been reading Anglo-Saxon at Edinburgh University; yes, he had found Ballads in 1923 on that dreary trip to Orkney; but in the

1920s he doubted whether Scottish literature could ever become a national literature again, and belief in MacDiarmid's Scottish Literary Renaissance only came – and for a short time – with increasing illness. Indeed there is a paradoxical and inextricable link between his illness and his movement towards Scots poetry; an inverse ratio whereby as his physical condition deteriorates, his need for the only possible consolation for a man of his intelligent honesty increases.

That possibility lay in embedding himself and his predicament within the tradition of his peers, the Makars from the distant past down to MacDiarmid in the present, and within the shared and recorded experience in proverb, anecdote, song and legend. To do this, Soutar had to accelerate a process of growth from innocence to experience which was the organising principle behind the linked categories of Riddle, Bairnrhyme, Whigmaleerie, and Scots poetry.

The Riddles are poetry; like so much of Soutar's work, based on an unusual, fragmented and lateral creative approach which refuses to impose false unity of form. Written for Evelyn, nevertheless they disturbingly include as topics, amongst rainbows and soap-bubbles, beard, echo, shadow, skull, dream, cuckoo, and 'the child you were'. Turn after enjoying them to the Bairnrhymes, and poems like 'The Daft Tree' (1931) and 'The Wind' (1943) show how Soutar has worked with the idea of Riddle reversed, as an essence now developed, with the same essential quirkiness and wonder, but approached not through challenge to the reader but through lateral association. That is to say that one grows into the other; and similarly, amidst Bairnrhymes like 'Bausy Broon' (1930) wonderfully suited to children, there regularly occur some extremely unchildlike and sardonic comments on human frailty. Henryson's influence is seen everywhere, as in 'The Herryin o' Jenny Wren' (1932), a sophisticated Scots 'Who Killed Cock Robin?'; and comedy and tragedy are grotesque partners in poems like 'Wish' (1942) and 'Lauch When You Can' (1943). Is the Unicorn-linked 'The Hunt' (1941) really for children?

And the Whigmaleeries likewise – at a higher level – burst their apparent bounds. Real grimness and mature ironic comment, managed with consummate craft, suggest that separation of many, if not all these poems, into a category which implies that the poet is indulging himself in fantasy and cantrips, is to demean their achievement. The Japanese legend-poem, 'The Wood' (1937) goes far beyond mere fanciful escapism; 'The Hungry Mauchs' of the same year is a thinly-disguised and grotesque Worm-poem; 'The Hungry Toon' (1940) is similarly disguised social anger, akin to the English Symbol, with its terrible imagery of 'wizzent bairns like auld men'; and there's extremely sophisticated satire on Scotland in 'Second Childhood' (1942) – at J M Barrie's expense – and 'Hal o' the Wynd' (1943).

As in his epigrams, Soutar could be devastatingly sardonic ironic regarding what and whom he sees as spurious and immoral in Scottish tradition. In the first poem Barrie is seen as both a fitting and unfit representative of a 'sair forjaskit mother', Scotland, and in the second the 'hero' of Scott's Fair Maid of Perth who didn't really care who he killed, since either side of the battle was alike to him, is identified as a type of Scottish history and its endless internecine strife.

And with poems of the stature of 'Far Awa in Araby' and 'King Worm' it's obvious that the distinction between Whigmaleerie and mature Scots poem has vanished. It remains for Soutar's personal and creative renaissance to go beyond vision and dream, Gowks and Unicorns, to discover something beyond despair and a willed commitment to politics or pacifism.

'Scotland' (1938) shows how far Soutar has moved from the nation-affirmation of 'The Auld Tree', and 'The Whale'. Beginning with the visionary stance of the poet, who 'sees whaur he canna see', as in the earlier poems, the poet now sees a very different Scotland of unrest and unsureness, with 'sauls that are stark and nesh' and 'sauls that wud dree the day'. Soutar's core-symbolism has gone. This difficult and ambiguous poem marks a withdrawal from the desire to be identified with the

New Scotland, instead asking the reader to find – whatever it turns out to be, mean or great – their own Scotland. The poet concludes:

> It is owre late for fear:
> Owre early for disclaim;
> When ye come hameless here
> And ken ye are at hame.

VI

Just over a week before he died, Soutar's diary entry for Wednesday, 6 October 1943 observes, with powerful and moving imagery, what has been lost and accepted, as well as what seemed most valuable and enduring in the life he was leaving:

> 'The other evening it came to me almost as a relief that for many months the attractiveness of women no longer disturbed me; that neither in dream or day-dream was I fretted by images of passion. Everything in my life is being quieted; and the great orbit of life is moving in from the bounds of the universe like the gradually diminishing circle of light from a wasting flame. Whether the mood adapts itself to the changing environment, or whether I have somehow achieved a sense of proportion which adapts itself readily to the inevitable, I am scarcely touched by regret or anxiety; but derive even an element of satisfaction from being able to stand back and watch myself busied or idling under the shadow of a doom which is but rarely remembered. So much can wither away from the human spirit and yet the great gift of the ordinary day remains: the stability of the small things of life which yet in their constancy are the greatest. All the daily kindness; the little obligations, the signs of remembrance in the homely gifts: these do not pass, but still hearten the body and spirit to the verge of the grave.'

John Soutar left his house to Perth Town Council, in memory of his late wife and son. The conditions are simple. The council should retain the house in its present position 'and maintain the plaque referring to my son's residence in the house which is at present on the east or front wall of the said house.' The council could not sell the house and 'the room on the ground floor of the said house in which my son spent the last fourteen years of his life confined to bed shall be shown to any interested person or persons who may apply to the said Lord Provost, Magistrates and Councillors to be shown the room and that at all reasonable times.'

The plaque was unveiled on what would have been the poet's sixtieth birthday. The platform party photographed in front of the house were Perth Provost John Buchan, John Soutar, Dr D.B.Low, Soutar's school friend and former doctor, Helen B.Cruickshank and Rev John Kitchen, minister of the North Church, Perth. The crowd spilled on to the street. A press photograph shows MacDiarmid as a face in the crowd.

The plaque was erected by John Soutar as part of a campaign to preserve his son's memory and to keep his name before the public. It describes William Soutar as 'The Scottish Poet'. His manuscripts, notes and letters were left to the National Library of Scotland and he bequeathed his son's library to Perth and Kinross County Library service. John Soutar commissioned the 1948 edition of Soutar's *Collected Poems*, edited by Hugh MacDiarmid, and also commissioned Alexander Scott's critical biography *Still Life* and provided 'every assistance, encouragement and kindness during the preparation of *Diaries of a Dying Man*.

VII

As W. R. Aitken found, the ordering of Soutar's poems is an extremely difficult business. Soutar categorised his poems into Bairnsangs, Poems in Scots, Whigmaleeries an the like. Any suggestion of reconciling these differing categories with the dates or order of creation were never satisfactory. Indeed such efforts are ultimately restricting and offer what we believe to be a distorted view of the range of Soutar's poetry. We have therefore cut the knot and given the poems an order which we hope will show their remarkable scope and vitality. Any reader wishing to gain an idea of Soutar's development can, we believe, gain that from this introduction.

Finally, it was a matter of great regret that the editors were unable to include a sample of Soutar's magnificent translations which cover a range of poets from William Blake to Boris Pasternak and include ancient Irish, Chinese and Japanese texts as well as European folk songs.

Into a Room

selected poems of William Soutar

Yon Day

I lang for yon day whan I'll be a loon
And naebody to daur me;
Wi' a fare-ye-weel to this auld, grey toun;
And the weys o' the world afore me.

The beckin boat wil be ready to rin
That winna gang without me:
The flotterin flüde will be rowin in,
And the white birds wavin about me.

And I'll sing the sangs o' the sailor-men
Wi' the spindrift fleein owre me:
And the fremmit lands sae far frae my ain
Will fraith oot o' the fame afore me.

---

lang: long; loon: lad; daur: dare; flotterin flüde: lapping tide;
fremmit: foreign; fraith: froth

The Tryst

O luely, luely cam she in
And luely she lay doun:
I kent her be her caller lips
And her breists sae sma' and roun'.

A' thru the nicht we spak nae word
Nor sinder'd bane frae bane:
A' thru the nicht I heard her hert
Gang soundin' wi' my ain.

It was about the waukrife hour
Whan cocks begin to craw
That she smool'd saftly thru the mirk
Afore the day wud daw.

Sae luely, luely, cam she in
Sae luely was she gaen
And wi' her a' my simmer days
Like they had never been.

---

luely: quietly, softly; **caller**: fresh; **sinder'd**: sundered;
waukrife: wakening, wakeful; **smool'd**: slipped

Nae Day Sae Dark

Nae day sae dark; nae wüd sae bare;
Nae grund sae stour wi' stane;
But licht comes through; a sang is there;
A glint o' grass is green.

Wha hasna thol'd his thorter'd hours
And kent, whan they were by,
The tenderness o' life that fleurs
Rock-fast in misery?

Song

Whaur yon broken brig hings owre;
Whaur yon water maks nae soun';
Babylon blaws by in stour:
Gang doun wi' a sang, gang doun.

Deep, owre deep, for onie drouth:
Wan eneuch an ye wud droun:
Saut, or seelfu', for the mouth;
Gang doun wi' a sang, gang doun.

Babylon blaws by in stour
Whaur yon water maks nae soun':
Darkness is your only door;
Gang doun wi' a sang, gang doun.

---

stour: dust; **thol'd**: suffered; **thorter'd**: thwarted; **drowth**:
thirst; **eneuch**: enough; **saut**: punishment; **seelfu'**: pleasant

Yesterday

I'm auld eneuch noo
To be the faither o' yon deid bairn
That was me.
It was the sicht o' the wild-rose
That minded me o't.
Monie a simmer's day, whan it was owre hot
To breenge eftir a butterflee
Or rin wi' a gird,
I ligg'd at the brae-fit and heard
The bee's and the burn's sang;
And the gowk croodlin' fae the wüds abüne.
And as I gaed hame
I'd pou the sma', wild roses
And fling them awa, or lang;
They were deid sae süne.

The Keekin-Gless

Lassie at the keekin-gless
Ye arena there yoursel';
Owre ilka shüther is a face
That comes to keek as weel.

Lassie at the keekin-gless
Ye aye maun look on three:
The dead face, and the livin face,
And the ane that is to be.

---

breenge: lunge, move carelessly; **gird**: hoop; **ligg'd**: lay;
brae-fit: foot of the hill; **abüne**: above; **ilka**: each; **shüther**:
shoulder; **aye**: always; **maun**: must; **ane**: one

The Makar

Nae man wha loves the lawland tongue
But warsles wi' the thocht –
There are mair sangs that bide unsung
Nor a' that hae been wrocht.

Ablow the wastrey o' the years,
The thorter o' himsel',
Deep buried in his bluid he hears
A music that is leal.

And wi' this lealness gangs his ain;
And there's nae ither gait
Though a' his feres were fremmit men
Wha cry: *Owre late, owre late.*

Evening Star

Lift up your e'en and greet nae mair,
The black trees on the brae are still;
And lichtsome, in the mirkl'd air,
A star gangs glaidly owre the hill.

Sae far awa fae worldly soun'
In laneliness it glimmers by;
And the cauld licht comes kindly doun
On earth and a' her misery.

---

warsles: wrestles, struggles; **wrocht**: brought about;
wastrey: waste; **thorter**: failure, waste; **leal**: real, true;
feres: comrades; **fremmit**: foreign; **mirkl'd**: darkened

The Halted Moment

Wha hasna turn'd inby a sunny street
And fund alang its length nae folk were there:
And heard his step fa' steadily and clear
Nor wauken ocht but schedows at his feet.
Shüther to shüther in the reemlin heat
The houses seem'd to hearken and to stare;
But a' were doverin whaur they stüde and were
Like wa's ayont the echo o' time's beat.
Wha hasna thocht whan atween stanes sae still,
That had been biggit up for busyness,
He has come wanderin into a place
Lost, and forgotten, and unchangeable:
And thocht the far-off traffic sounds to be
The weary waters o' mortality.

---

wauken: waken; **ocht**: anything; **shüther**: shoulder; **reemlin**: trembling, shimmering; **doverin**: dozing; **ayont**: beyond

The Room

Into the quiet of this room
Words from the clamorous world come:
The shadows of the gesturing year
Quicken upon the stillness here.

The wandering waters do not mock
The pool within its wall of rock
But turn their healing tides and come
Even as the day into this room.

A Summer Morning

Earth is so lovely at this hour
That every dull stone
Seems, in the generous light, to have grown
Alert; a sentient thing
Which joys, even as every flower
Seems joyous and would loosen from its stem
To float with butterflies on fragrant wing:
And no less happy is the man who stares
On stone and flower; and unawares,
Like to a god, is blessed and blesses them.

The Apparition

There she is halted by the hedge again:
Only a shade out of the shadowy day?
Only a shape of leafage between the grey
Twilight and the grey drift of the small rain?
Her skirt is green; her coat is darker green:
Are these the bones of her face, are these the stray
Clusters of her glimmering hair; or the way
The pale light lingers on the leaves' wet sheen?
There she is halted by the hedge again:
There she is risen again out of the ground:
She is looking this way; and in the rain
Her lips are open but there is no sound:
Only a shape of leafage; only the grey
Shade of a shade; only the shadowy day?

Beyond the Garden

Beyond the garden is the town;
Beyond the town the furrow'd shire;
And still beyond – that world unknown
Is waiting for the traveller.

Pity the mind which has grown old
Beside its youth; and in old age
Can share but memories which hold
The pilgrim from his pilgrimage.

Cosmos

There is a universe within this room
Where, through the half-swung shutters,
The sundering day has thrust
A wall of light between the darkened walls:
And on and on and on monotonously
The ticking tongue of time stutters
Across the silence and the dust
Which falls, drifted in little worlds,
From gloom to gloom.

Sunny Shower

The drops of liquid light which fall from air
And sparkling everywhere:
Blackbird and thrush, these listening poachers,
Now as they forage, crush
The fragile jewels glistening on the grass.
Hedges are made of glass;
And, in the hush, a wall of crystal stone;
Which shatters with no sound
When the wind, in a rush, lays a rough hand thereon
And is over at a bound.

The Moment

Between the crowing of the cock
Love is fulfilled and is forlorn:
Between the clicking of the clock
A star dies and a star is born.

Between the beating of the breast
Love is fulfilled and is forlorn:
Between the wave and the wave-crest
Is meeting and is no return.

Backlands

In backlands aff the Ropey Close,
Whan the müne grows cauld and sneep,
The bairnies wha were beddit boss
Hae grat themsel's to sleep.

The auld wife, boo'd abüne her wark,
Steeks on be cannel-flame:
The sma'-hour dinnles through the dark;
The trollop taivers hame.

Gin Ye Had Come Last Nicht

Gin ye had come last nicht
Wi' the thochts o' ye that cam',
Ye wudna noo be what ye are
Nor I be what I am.

Gin ye had come last nicht,
Whan my thocht was but ae thocht,
It wud hae been anither sang
That you an' I had wrocht.

---

sneep: white; **boss**: empty; **grat**: cried; **boo'd**: bowed;
abüne: above; **steeks**: stitches; **dinnles**: vibrates;
trollop: gangly person; **taivers**: wanders; **gin**: if; **wrocht**: made

The Gowk

Half doun the hill, whaur fa's the linn
Far frae the flaught o' fowk,
I saw upon a lanely whin
A lanely singin' gowk:
Cuckoo, cuckoo;
And`at my back
The howie hill stüde up and spak;
Cuckoo, cuckoo.

There was nae soun': the loupin' linn
Hung frostit in its fa':
Nae bird was on the lanely whin
Sae white wi' fleurs o' snaw:
Cuckoo, cuckoo;
I stüde stane still;
And saftly spak the howie hill:
Cuckoo, cuckoo.

---

linn: waterfall; **flaught**: bustle; **whin**: stone; **loupin'**: leaping

The Dark Thocht

Up on the hill abüne the toun
Whan pit-mirk is the nicht,
And but a star or twa glent doun
Wi' their cauld and clinty licht;

A thocht comes cryin through the bluid
That there is nae toun ava:
Only the water and the wüd
And the heuch attowre them a':

And set within a nicht sae black,
And in sae lane an hour,
Wha kens gin he is glowerin back
Or glimmerin far afore?

The Quiet Comes In

Whan the rage is by
The bluid grows still:
Whan the tears are dry
The bairn sleeps weel.

Whan the roch winds low'r
Sangsters begin:
Whan the sang is owre
The quiet comes in.

---

pit-mirk: deep darkness; **clinty**: hard; **heuch**: cliff; **attowre**: over

Genethliac Chant

This is the day whan I was born:
Tak pity on my mither:
I hae the saul o' a unicorn:
Tak pity on my faither.

I micht hae learn'd a handy trade:
Tak pity on the lairish:
But I'm a penniless poet instead:
Tak pity on the parish.

I micht hae bade a briny boy:
Tak pity on my hurdies:
I micht hae been somebody's joy:
Tak pity on the birdies.

The wind blaws north and the wind blaws south
Wi' naither brank nor brechin:
The Lord has pit a sang in the mouth
That micht hae been a sechin.

---

lairish: teachers, the learnéd; **bade**: remained;
briny: bold, cheery; **hurdies**: buttocks; **brank**: bridle;
brechin: harness; **sechin**: sighing

Silence

The hert may be sae rowth wi' sang
It has nae need to sing;
The e'en sae lichtit as owregang
The sicht o' oniething:

Like ane wha in a carefree hour
Frae Saturn micht look furth
Wi' nocht but brichtness reemlin owre
Atween him and the earth:

A' the roch rammage o' the world
Dwin'd to a dinnlin bell:
A' the dark warsle o' the world
Ingether'd and stane-still.

---

rowth: full, abundant; **owregang**: exceed;
ingether'd: ingathered

The Grief that Gangs Far Ben

Whan we're nae langer pin'd
Be gledness that has gaen:
And sairest stounds hae dwin'd
Frae the dourest dird taen:

Whan we hae sma' regret
For a' that we hae tin'd,
There is a sadness yet
Bides waukrife in the mind:

A shame that gaed far in
And canna be untwin'd:
Cauld comfort said or düne
That micht hae been sae kind.

Whan Gledness Has Grown Grey

Tak thocht that in a hundred years
A body no unlike yoursel
Will ken a gledness whan he hears
The gowk cry on the hamely hill.

And whan your ain joy has grown grey,
And sma's the comfort for your care,
Ca' ben the thocht o' yon far day
Bricht in the gowd and green o' the year.

---

stounds: blows; **dwin'd**: fade away; **dourest**: most stubborn;
dird: blow; **tin'd**: lost; **waukrife**: wakeful;
ca' ben: call in; **gowd**: gold

The Wind

He's lowse, he's lowse, yon wowffin tyke
That yammers through the scudderin wüd:
Taks at a lowp baith burn and dyke,
And ranters on be onie road.

Sae waukrife whan the nicht comes in
He yowls up frae the vennel'd toun,
Whaur yon auld baudrons far abüne
Wi' glittery e'e is glaikin doun.

---

wowffin: barking; **tyke**: dog; **baudrons**: cats;
glaikin: glancing

King Worm

What care I for kirk or state?
What care I for war's alarm?
A' are beggars at my yett:
I am King Worm.

Aye a getherin girst I get;
A lippen hairst at time o' hairm:
Want and wastrey mak me fat:
I am King Worm.

The hale world is my heapit plate,
And death the flunkey at my airm:
Wha sae merry owre his meat?
I am King Worm.

---

yett: gate; **girst**: mill payment in kind; **lippen**: dependable;
hairst: harvest; **flunkey**: servant

Consolation

Saftly about her darg she gaed
Nor thocht o' richt or wrang;
Sae nesh the body on the bed
Like it wud wauk or lang.

A neebour woman cam in-by
Whan day was nearly düne;
She spak nae word o' misery
Nor look'd wi' troubl'd e'en.

She bade or mirkl'd was the west
And the müne was lifted owre;
Syne laid a hand on the ither's breist
And gaed ayont the door.

---

darg: work; **nesh**: soft; **lang**: lie long; **bade**: stayed;
mirkl'd: darkened; **syne**: since

Scotland

Atween the world o' licht
And the world that is to be
A man wi' unco sicht
Sees whaur he canna see:

Gangs whaur he canna walk:
Recks whaur he canna read:
Hauds what he canna tak:
Mells wi' the unborn dead.

Atween the world o' licht
And the world that is to be
A man wi' unco sicht
Monie a saul maun see:

Sauls that are sterk and nesh:
Sauls that wud dree the day:
Sauls that are fain for flesh
But canna win the wey.

Hae ye the unco sicht
That sees atween and atween
This world that lowes in licht:
Yon world that hasna been?

It is owre late for fear,
Owre early for disclaim;
Whan ye come hameless here
And ken ye are at hame.

---

unco: unusual; **recks**: takes heed; **mells**: mixes; **maun**: must;
sterk: stark; **nesh**: tender; **dree**: endure; **fain**: desire;
lowes: glows

The Earth Hings Like A Keekin'-Glass

The earth hings like a keekin'-glass,
Upon the wa' o' nicht,
And there the sin wud see himsel'
Stüde up in his ain licht.

Outby the levin's langest loup
The earth's sma' skinkles rin:
But wha is yon that sklents attour
The shüther o' the sin?

Fleurs Frae the Rock

Fleurs frae the rock:
Sae cannie fa' the shoo'rs;
Sae straucht the shock o' the sun-smert:
O life the hert is yours
An ye brak the hert.

---

sin: sun; **levin**: lightning; **loup**: leap; **skinkles**: gleams;
rin: run; **sklents**: looks askance; **attour**: beyond;
cannie: crafty; **shoo'rs**: shores; **straucht**: straight

Apotheosis

Afore the world, like a frostit stane,
Birls on thru space;
Afore the sin has gaen black in the face,
And the nicht ligg's in the lift
And winna shift;
Lang, lang afore the hinmaist skelter o' snaw
Dings and dings in a yowdendrift
That faulds, like the dounfa'
O time's cauld mort-claith, round the deid yird –
Man sall tak wings;
And, as a bird, flee owre the wa' o' the world
To bigg his nest in the braid breist
O' Cassiopeia
Or whaur the galaxy hings like a watergaw
Lippen on nae sin.

Lang, lang, or earth's day is düne
Man sall tak wings
And lauch at the auld-farand blethers
O' gowdan feathers;
And lauch, and lauch, while his bluid sings,
Abüne the gaunch o' the thunner,
And the deid sterns ane be ane
Whunner by like flauchts frae a cleckin-stane.

---

birls: spins; **ligg**: lie; **hinmaist**: last; **skelter**: rush;
dings: beats; **yowdendrift**: wind-driven snow; **mort-claith**:
coffin-cloth; **bigg**: build; **braid**: broad; **watergaw**: rainbow;
lippen: dependent; **auld-farand**: old-fasioned; **abüne**: above;
gaunch: snarl; **sterns**: stars; **whunner**: whizz; **flauchts**: flashes;
frae: from; **cleckin'-stane**: cracking stone

The Unicorn

When from the dark the day is born
Life's glory walks in white:
Upon the hills the unicorn
Glitters for mortal sight.

Out of their dream the hunters wake
With brightness on their eyes:
The foolish hurry forth to take,
But gently go the wise.

They only are the wise who claim
This for their foolishness:
To love the beast they cannot tame
Yet cheer the unending chase.

Wintry Beauty

Even in winter earth is lovely still,
Bared almost to the bone:
The clean anatomy of tree and hill;
The honesty of stone:

In ultimate endurance under the touch
Of fingering wind and frost:
Withered into a beauty beyond smutch
When all but all is lost:

An incorruptible and patient grace
From bravery forsworn:
The steadfastness upon an agéd face
Out of long sufferance born.

Simple Aveu

Now that I know you shall no longer move
About your garden,
And I no longer raise my arm in greeting
(It was our only meeting –
This far salute)
I may write down your love.
Few lines, in truth, can all its acts compute:
How you would hesitantly halt beside a flower
Knowing my eyes were on you,
And that our far greeting,
In the next moment, would be flung
Across the silence of the separating air:
This you would tell me frankly; unaware
Your body spoke to me:
You were so young.

The Permanence of the Young Men

No man outlives the grief of war
Though he outlive its wreck:
Upon the memory a scar
Through all his years will ache.

Hopes will revive when horrors cease;
And dreaming dread be stilled;
But there shall dwell within his peace
A sadness unannulled.

Upon his world shall hang a sign
Which summer cannot hide:
The permanence of the young men
Who are not by his side.

In the Time of Tyrants

All that the hand may touch;
All that the hand may own;
Crumbles beyond time's clutch
Down to oblivion.

Fear not the boasts which wound:
Fear not the threats which bind:
Always on broken ground
The seeds fall from the mind.

Always in darkness loam
A birthday is begun;
And from its catacomb
A candle lights the sun.

Who Are These Children?

With easy hands upon the rein,
And hounds at their horses' feet,
The ladies and the gentlemen
Ride through the village street.

Brightness of blood upon the coats
And on the women's lips:
Brightness of silver at the throats
And on the hunting whips.

Is there a day more calm, more green
Under this morning hour;
A scene more alien than this scene
Within a world at war?

Who are these children gathered here
Out of the fire and smoke
That with remembering faces stare
Upon the foxing folk?

He Who Weeps for Beauty Gone

He who weeps for beauty gone
Hangs about his neck a stone.

He who mourns for this lost youth
Daily digs a grave for truth.

He who prays for happy hours
Tramples upon earthy flowers.

He who asks an oath from love
Doth thereby his folly prove.

Mourn not overmuch, nor stress
After love or happiness.

He who weeps for beauty gone
Stoops to pluck a flower of stone.

The Earth Abides

When our loud days are chronicles
Of rancour and revenge
Whoever walks upon these hills
Shall not remember change.

He shall be moulded by their mood:
Their granite and their grass
Through secret ways of sense and blood
Into his life will pass.

And he shall love his native land;
And still an exile be
If in its name he lift a hand
To smite an enemy.

And he shall look upon the sun
And see his ensign there
If earth belong to all, and none;
Gifted as light and air.

From the Wilderness

He who was driven into the wilderness
Is now come back from misery to bless
The hounding spirit.
He who was rich and now so seeming poor
Owns an inheritance which was not his before –
Even his self.
This was the gift from the dark hour which thrust
Him forth to solitude;
Which laid him in a grave while yet the dust
Was under him; while yet the blood
Watered the withering verge twixt sense and sand.
He knew the hour of nothingness when the hand
Is empty, and empty is the heart;
And the intelligence, with its keen dart
Of reasonable speech, slays its own pride.
'Twas thus he died;
Suffering his solitary hour beyond the world of men:
And it was thus, alone, he found the flower
Of his own self;
Which yet had been only a flower of stone
Had he not brought it back into the world again.

The Turn of the Year

This is the day of change
And this the hour;
The wind is holding its breath.
Each flower looks downward to the earth
As in a stare.
The listening air stands still:
Only the stream, like a bright chattering child,
Is unaware of the foreboding peace.
This is the day, the hour,
And now the very moment fills the sky;
While the undreaming earth,
Within a trice which measures a surcease,
Is paused upon a sigh.
Life lifts a hand to turn his hour-glass round:
A leaf,
A withered world is falling with no sound.

Stillness

Within my garden, and alone,
So still it was I seemed to hear
The beetle crawl across the stone.

I seemed to hear, deep in the erd,
The smooth worm groping for the light:
I seemed: nay, I am sure I heard.

And I am sure I heard the sound
Of dead leaves breaking from their boughs
And the low echo on the ground.

So still it was with not a trace
Of wind; save when the lazy moth
Churned a slow wave across my face.

But my own being stood apart
Still hearing in this earthy peace
The loud pulsation of its heart.

I had forgotten that the stone,
Whereon the noisy beetle stirred,
Was fallen from an age long gone.

I had forgotten that the leaf
Dropped from is bough; as from the mind
Our memories of joy or grief.

I had forgotten; but the chime
Of my own heart, with measured sound,
Fretted the stillness into time.

The Swallow

There are three Greeks upon a piece of stone
Who turn their heads and stare into the sky
While a young lad, with right hand lifted high,
Points to a bird which suddenly had flown
Above them, and beyond them, and is grown
Most small before the arm could range the eye
Or the round mouth unshape its quickening cry:
It is the swallow, look, ere it be gone!
Here, though the hands are dust, the sculptor's knife
Still wounds the heart to give it utterance
Naming a truth that each must make his own:
Ah! look, it is the swallow; and is life
That flies for ever from the dark mischance
Towards which man must turn naked, alone.

At Peace

Lighted leaves on the tree:
A wind not rough but strong:
Smoothly across their foamless sea
The clouds are blown along.

What world were lovelier?
I am content to cease
From mortal busyness and stare
Silent, alone, at peace.

The Arch

The days of our life are a bridge
Between night and night:

And we look not on eternity
But upon its light

Broken into beauty, by the day
And the life of men,

As the day is broken on the world's edge
By the falling rain.

The Return of the Swallow

We men who die
Feel the quick pulse of joy flood through the heart
When suddenly you dart
Across the sky.
Slowly the frail leaf, as a butterfly,
Breaks the imprisoning bud:
And, from the copse,
The cuckoo's parlance, in a singing sigh,
Slowly drops;
But you are swift;
And the flash of your wing on the eye
Startles the blood.
You are the moment of our entering
Into the spring:
Our leap from wintry barrenness to birth:
Our pledge from earth
That yet again we stand where we have stood.
O happy mood;
O happy, happy mood in which we are
Bodies that stare
As time's wing cleaves a wave-crest of life's flood.

Beyond Loveliness

High on the hillside,
Where the rough track enters the wood,
I sat in the sun;
The noonday silence, like an earthy mood
Over and about me,
Wove through the sense with the warm smell of grass.
I was content; and had forgot to brood
Forgetting my own mind:
'Earth's beauty is enough,' I said:
'And I at one, within this solitude,
Sharing a sunny stillness
Which lingers as a wind
Between the branches of the blood.'
And it was then that an old man trudged by
Bearing his pack of sticks:
He had no eye for nature; and his track
Was downward to the town:
With him my thought went down
As I was minded of man's misery,
And that the way he journeyed was my own.

Illumination

Those leaves of light, against the sky,
Which now the trees wears for a crown
Shine in a world behind the eye
Where winter cannot pull them down.

Eden is there and no leaf falls;
Or falling ever floats through light:
Fond fool! already on the walls
Is frost, and on the bough is blight.

Yet is the mind of man a tree
Whose sun is centre to the sun;
An eye eternal which can see
The forest in the burning stone.

The Whale

As I walk't by the Firth o' Forth,
Sae lately in the nicht,
There was nae man stüde at my side
Tae name yon antrin sicht.

Oot o' the midmaist deep it rax't
Whan saftly low'd the müne;
An' it was braid, an' unco lang,
An' the sea cam rowin' in.

Afore its breist the waters brak
As roond a wa' o' rocks:
Its broos were birslin i' the air
Abüne the weather-cocks.

An', as a fountain, frae its heid
Gaed up a waterspoot
Like it wud loup attour the müne
An' draik the sma sternes oot.

It cam straucht on wi' muckle mou
Wide gaunted like a pit;
An' the strang souffin' o' its braith
Sookit me intill it.

The whummlin' flood gaed ower my croun;
An' wi' a thunner-crack
The braid portcullis o' its chouks
Cam doun ahint my back.

---

antrin: strange; **rax't**: stretched; **low'd**: glowed;
braid: broad; **unco**: very; **broos**: brows; **abüne**: above;
draik: drench; **sternes**: stars; **gaunted**: yawned;
souffin: sighing; **whummlin'**: overturning; **chouks**: jaws;

Ben in the bodie o' the baest
It was nor day nor nicht,
For a' the condies o' its bluid
Low'd wi' a laich, reid licht.

I daunner'd here, I daunner'd there,
Thru vennel, wynd, an' pen';
An' aye the licht was roond aboot
An' aye I daunner'd ben.

I walkit on the lee-lang day,
I micht hae walkit twa,
Whan, a' at aince, I steppit oot
Intae a guidly schaw.

Ane eftir ane stüde ferny trees,
Purple an' gowd an' green;
An' as the wrak o' watergaws
The fleurs fraith'd up atween.

I wud hae minded nocht ava
O' the ferlie I was in
But aye the engine o' its hairt
Gaed stoundin far abüne;
An' whan it gien an' unco stert
The licht loup't in my een.

Lang, lang, I gowkit thru the trees
Nor livin thing saw I,
Till wi' a soundless fling o' feet
Unyirdly baes breez'd by.

---

ben: in; **condies**: conduits; **low'd**: glowed; **laich**: low; **daunner'd**:
wandered; **vennel**: alley; **pen**: archway; **lee-land**: sheltered land;
schaw: wood; **wrak**: ruin: **watergaws**: rainbows; **fraith'd**: frothed;
ferlie: wonder; **stounding**: beating, throbbing; **gien**: gave; **unco**:
unusual; **gowkit**: gawped; **unyirdly**: unearthly; **baes**: beasts;

They flisk't an' flung'd an' flirn'd aboot
An' fluther'd roond an' roond,
But nae leaf liftit on the tree
An' nae fit made a sound.

An' some had heids o' stags an' bulls,
An' breists o' serpent scales:
An' some had eagles' wings an' een,
An' some had dragons' tails.

An' ilka baest was gowd, or green,
Or purple like the wud,
But ae strang-bodied unicorn
That was as reid as bluid.

Then was I minded o' a tale
That I had lang forgat;
Hoo, the afore auld Noah's ark
Hunker'd on Ararat,

A muckle ferlie o' the deep,
That had come up tae blaw,
Gowpit abüne the shoglin' boat
An' haik't some baes awa.

Here, sin the daith o' the auld world,
They dwalt like things unborn;
An' I was wae for my ain land
Twin'd o' its unicorn.

I stüde like ane that has nae pou'r
An' yet, within a crack,
My hauns were on the unicorn
An' my bodie owre its back.

---

fit: foot; **hunker'd**: squatted; **muckle**: great; **ferlie**: wonder;
gowpit: gulped; **shoglin'**: rocking; **haik't**: carried off;
wae: woe; **twin'd**: parted; **pou'r**: power;

Wi' ae loup it had skail'd the wud,
An' wi anither ane
'Twas skelpin' doun the gait I'd cam
Thru vennel, wynd an' pen'.

Süne was I waur that I cud sense
The soundin' o' the sea;
An' that the licht o' my ain world
Cam round me cannily.

On, an' aye on, thru whistlin wind
We flang in fuddert flicht;
An' louder was the waff o' waves,
An' lichter was the licht.

Owre ilka sound I hear the stound
O' the loupin' waterspoot,
An' as it loupt the sea-baest gowp't
An' the unicorn sprang oot:
Aye, straucht atween the sinderin' chouks
The unicorn sprang oot.

It steppit thru the siller air,
For day was at the daw;
An' what had been a bluid-reid baest
Was noo a baest o' snaw.

Or lang, my fit was by the Forth
Whaur I had stüde afore;
But the unicorn gaed his ain gait
An' as he snoov'd owre Arthur's Sate
I heard the lion roar.

---

skail'd: cleared, scaled; **skelpin'**: galloping; **gait**: way;
waur: aware; **cannily**: gently; **flang**: flew; **fuddert**: rushing;
waff: waft; **sinderin'**: parting; **siller**: silver;
snoov'd: steadily moved

Why the Worm Feeds on Death

There was a burn fae Paradise
That smoor'd itsel' in sand
Ayont the border o' the bents
That raik'd round Adam's land.

Here Cain drave in the reekin' nowt
To slochan fae the plew:
Here Abel herded sheep and kye
Whaur the carse-clover grew.

And here a' day and ilka day,
Broggin ablow the grass,
Back and fore be the caller burn
The warslin' worms wud pass.

It was their wark that lows'd the yird
And lat the burn souk in:
It was their wark that mirl'd the mools
To hap the seed abüne:
It was the warplin' o' their wark
That wrocht a deadly sin.

---

smoor'd: smothered; **bents**: coarse grasses; **raik'd**: ranged;
reekin': steaming; **nowt**: cattle; **slochan**: slake; **kye**: cattle; **carse**:
cress; **broggin**: piercing; **caller**: fresh; **warslin'**: struggling;
lows'd: loosened; **yird**: earth; **mirl'd**: crumbled; **mools**: fine soil;
hap: cover; **warplin'**: warping; **wrocht**: wrought;

Ootby the drums o' Paradise
This was the wrang they wrocht:
Nae langer be the caller burn
Water o' life they socht:
Nae langer, birz'd ablow the braird,
Water o' life they brocht.

But a' about the rivin' rits
They howder'd in their drouth;
And smool'd awa the mervy pith
Wi' monie a mauchy mouth:
Or corn and bere were in a dwine
Though the weet sloung'd fae the south.

Cain glunsh'd attour his faither's fields
That meisl'd, day and day,
Whaur yet the onding drung in dubs
Abüne the clappit clay.

'O we hae düne some waefu' wrang
Afore the sicht o' God
And we maun graith a haly-place
To sain our cankert sod.'

He ca'd his brither; and they bigg'd
Twa altars stane on stane:
And Abel brocht a snaw-white lamb
But there was nocht for Cain;
Nocht but the blashy braird abüne
The worms that were its bane.

---

birz'd: pushed; **ablow**: below; **braird**: young grain; **rivin'**:
twisting; **rits**: roots; **howder'd**: huddled; **drouth**: thirst; **smool'd**:
slipped; **mervy**: rich; **pith**: substance; **mauchy**: maggoty; **bere**:
barley; **dwine**: decline; **weet**: wet; **sloung'd**: drenched; **glunsh'd**:
sullenly slouched; **attour**: over; **meisl'd**: slowly wasted away;
onding: heavy snow fall, **drung**: lingered; **dubs**: puddles; **clappit**:
close-packed; **maun**: must; **graith**: make ready, **sain**: heal;
cankert: blighted; **bigg'd**: built; **blashy**: watery; **bane**: bone;

Spir'd up intill the mornin' air
Gaed Abel's haly lowe;
But Cain's, amang his wauchy wisps,
Smoor'd in a smochy drow.

Cain lookit wi' a stertl'd e'e
On Abel's luntin' licht;
Or a' his wrath roos'd, in a crack,
And straucht ahint his brither's back
He struck wi' mortal micht.

Was it the thunner, or God's cry,
Abüne the bluid-weet face
That drave him on, and far awa,
Thru monie a lanely place.

Was it the thocht o' yon clear burn,
And his ain faither's tent,
That brocht him, at the time o' hairst,
Back to the fields he kent.

Sma' words Cain and his faither spak,
And nocht o' what was by;
Though baith met on the grassy hauch
Whaur Abel herded kye.

Sma' words Cain and his mither spak,
And nocht o' what had been;
Though baith saw in the ither's face
The death that stüde atween.

---

spir'd: spiralled; **lowe**: flame: **wauchy**: feeble; **smoor'd**: hid;
smochy: sullen; **drow**: huff; **luntin'**: brightened; **roos'd**: aroused;
ahint: behind; **hairst**: harvest; **kent**: knew; **hauch**: low ground by
the river;

But on the morn, while yet the daw
Was streekin fae the strae,
Cain gaed ootby and socht the bing
Abüne his brither's clay.

Raw upon raw the growthy corn
Round the twa altars stüde,
And in the licht the gowdan girst
Hung doun like draps o' bluid.

Raw upon raw the birsy bere
Rax't up, sae routh and green.
Abüne the braid and sandy sheuch
Whaur the caller burn had been.

Cain ca'd his faither to his side,
For he was sairly fraist,
And speer'd what miracle cud mak
The blashy fields sae blest;
Sin baskit was the guidly burn
That wander'd to the waste.

'It was the God wha drave ye furth
And wha has brocht ye hame:
It was the body that ye brak
In yon stark hour o' grame:
It was the worms wha wrocht ye wrang
And smurl upon their shame.

---

daw: dawn; **strae**: straw; **bing**: heap; **raw**: row; **girst**: offering;
birsy: bristly; **rax't**: stretched; **routh**: abundant; **abüne**: above;
sheuch: trench; **sairly**: sorely; **fraist**: astonished; **speer'd**: asked;
sin: since; **baskit**: dried up; **grame**: passion; **smurl**: ate furtively;

'God saw the worms about the rit
Wha aince had glegly wrocht:
Nae langer be the caller burn
Water o' life they socht:
Nae langer, birz'd ablow the braid,
Water o' life they brocht.

'This was the deathliness sae dern
That kyth'd in deadly feud;
And wark'd a curse upon the worm
Wha mock'd the lifey flüde.

'And this the curse God set upon
The worms that lirk'd ae laith:
"Ye wha hae wal'd death out o' life
Sall wale life out o' death." '

Cain stüde outby a' time and place,
Like ane wha isna born,
Or he taen up his faither's heuk
And gaed amang the corn.

And as he swung the sinderin blade
He spak ablow his breath:
'Ye wha hae wal'd death out o' life
Sall wale life out o' death.'

Cain hairst the graith o' the gowdan field
As owre the heuk he boo'd;
Nor kent the merle was in the schaw,
The laverock in the clüde;
But as the weet ran doun his breist
He thoucht o' his brither's bluid.

---

glegly: nimbly; **dern**: secret; **kyth'd**: appeared; **lirk'd**: lay
hidden; **laith**: loathsome; **wal'd**: chosen; **sall**: shall; **or**: until;
boo'd: bowed; **merle**: blackbird; **schaw**: wood; **laverock**: skylark;
clude: cloud; **weet**: rain

The Auld Tree

(for Hugh McDiarmid)

There's monie a sicht we dinna see
Wi' oniething ye'd ca' an e'e:
There's monie a march o' fantoun grund
The forret fit has never fund:
And gin we tak nae yirdlin road
Our body, halflins corp and clod,
Sits steerless as a man o' stane
Unwarly that it is alane.
'Twas sic a body I had kent
Ae simmer mornin' whaur the bent
I ligg'd on, flichter'd a' its fleurs
Up to the lift: hours upon hours
My thowless banes fu' streekit were
Like ane unhappit frae his lair.
I heard nae mair the laverock's chitter
Nor crawin' corbie wi' a flitter
Gae up frae howkin': a' my sicht
Was rinnin' thru the reemlin' licht
And whitter'd yont that fleury brae
Without a sidlins gliff: a' day
My body ligg'd and but a breath
Hingin' atween itsel' and death.
It's no for makars to upvant
Themsel's; lat mummers mak a mant
O' a' their makins: what's to tell
Is mair nor oniebody's sel':
Is mair nor is the word that tells it;

---

fantoun: unearthly, fantastic; **forret**: forward; **gin**: if;
yirdlin: earthly; **halflins**: half and half; **corp**: corpse;
bent: coarse grass; **ligg'd**: lay; **flichter'd**: fluttered; **lift**: sky;
thowless: spiritless; **streekit**: laid out; **unhappit**: uncovered;
laverock: skylark; **corbie**: raven; **howkin'**: howking;
whitter'd: moved lightly; **yont**: beyond; **sidlins**: sideways;
gliff: moment; **makars**: poets; **upvant**: boast; **mant**: stutter;

And mair nor is the mind that spells it.
There is a tree that lifts its hands
Owre a' the worlds: and though it stands
Aye green abüne the heids o' men
Afttimes it's lang afore we ken
That it is there. Auld, auld, is it;
And was a tree or onie fit,
Nor God's, daunner'd in its saft schaw:
Nor sall it be a runt though the ca'
O' times hinnermaist sea dees doun
Intill a naething wi' nae soun'.
It's thramml'd deeper nor the pit
O' space, and a' our planets sit
As toad-stools crinin' whaur the rit
Raxes into the licht: owreheid
The heichest stern, like to a gleed
Blawn up, hings waukrifelie and waif
Nor lunts upon the laichest leaf.
Aye, monie a sicht we canna see
Wi' oniething ye'd ca' an e'e:
Yet maun the makar carry back
A ferlie that the e'en can tak;
And busk his roun-tree on the hill
In shape o' haly Yggdrasil.
There was a carl; it's lang sin he
Gowkit upon this eldren tree
Whaur thru the mornin' haar it boo'd
A rung owre earth's green solitude:
And there, ablow the sanctit schaw,
Baith bird and beastie and the sma'
Flitterin' fikies o' the air
Heez'd at a ca' – and they were there.
That's lang, lang syne; but at the yett

---

thramml'd: buried; **crinin'**: shrinking; **rit**: root; **raxes**: stretches;
gleed: spark; **lunts**: burns brightly; **laichest**: lowest; **ferlie**:
marvel, wonder; **busk**: dress; **carl**: old man; **sanctit**: sainted;
fikies: tiny creatures; **heez'd**: lifted up;

O' yon saft gairthen still is set
The challance o' the singin' word
That whunners like a lowin' sword.
Strauchtly I lookit, whaur the kennin'
O' that auld prophet aince was wennin,
And in ablow the haly tree
Noo sat, in crouse clanjampherie,
A' the leal makars o' the world.
Up thru the leaves their claivers skirl'd
The hale o' the day; nae rung but dirl'd
Wi' sang, or lauchter, or the diddle
O' flochtersome fife, and flute, and fiddle.
Some gate I slippit in mysel',
But ask na how – I canna tell,
And sittin' cheek-for-chow wi' Rab
I hearkint while he eas'd his gab
On him wha screed the *Sang to Davy*.
'Aye:' Rab was sayin': 'monie a shavie
Time ploys on man: just tak a gliff
Richt round – wha's here that seem'd nae cufe
In ither days: it maks a body
Nicher, like onie traikit cuddie,
To ken he's hame in spite o' a'
Was thocht his folly and his fa'.
Man, wha o' us, on lookin' back,
Sees ocht misgoggl'd, or wud tak
Ill-will at oniebody's flyte;
Nae doot the maist o' us gaed gyte,
But mebbe gyteness is the sweek
O' makin'. Hae anither keek
At a' our cronnies plankit saft

---

gairthen: garden; challance: challenge; whunners: thunders,
reverbarates; wennin: dwelling; crouse: merry; clanjampherie:
large gathering; leal: true; claivers: gossip; shavie: trick;
cufe: simpleton; nicher: snigger; traikit: wandering;
cuddie: donkey; misgoggl'd: misguided; flyte: verbal abuse;
gyte: mad; sweek: most artful way; plankit: set down;

Ablow this tree: a hantle's daft
Just like yoursel', and hardly ane
Hadna a wuddrum i' the bane.
I ken, I ken it's mair nor airms
And legs, or puckle harns and thairms
That maks a man: and weel I ken
Aft, or a man may win richt ben
To screenge his sel's sel', doun he snools
To death – but nane liggs in the mools:
Na, na; it's up and buskit and awa,
The earth's aye whummlin', aye the ca'
O' water jowin' to the müne:
The lang day's darg is never düne.
But aften times it's sair to dree
The fa'in o' braw fullyery
And the wagaein o' the bird:
What gin the hert ken, frae the yird,
Anither tree sall rax itsel'
And ither sangsters flee and mell
Intill its airms: what gin the hert
Ken weel the auld tree is a pairt
O' a' to come: time brocht its fa'
And, yonder, time maun rin awa.
O Scotland, whatna thistle rits
Into the mools; what bird noo sits
Whaur lang, lang syne there was a tree,
Younglin' and braw wi' fullyery,
Booin' its green and sternie croun
Abüne Dunbar and Henrysoun.
And I mysel' hae set a fit
Ablow a tree that rov'd its rit
Doun to the deid runt o' the auld;

---

hantle: fair number; **wuddrum**: madness; **puckle**: small amount;
harns: brains; **thairms**: intestines; **screenge**: discover; **liggs**: lies;
mools: the earth; **aft**: often; **jowin**: surging; **dree**: endure;
fullyery: foliage; **wagaein'**: departure; **gin**: if; **mell**: mingle;

But whatna rung noo lifts to fauld
The warblin' bird; what spatrels rin
Out on the four wings o' the win'.
Ah shairly, gin nae makar's breath
Blaw süne thru Scotland, doun to death
She'll gang and canker a' the world.
Owre lang her bastard sons hae skirl'd
Around the reid rose; wha sall name
The wild, sma' white-rose o' our hame.
Gin love were routh whaur nae hert socht;
Gin rhyme were fund whaur nae mind wrocht;
Gie me but ane frae oot this howff
And I'd wauk Scotland frae her souff.
O' wha wi' onie styme o' sang
Wud con her story and be lang
In liltin'; were it but to tell
It owre again to his ain sel'.'

Noo, as I harkint, I was waur
O' a lang stillness: and a haar
Cam owre me and nae mair I heard
O' sang, or minstrelsy, or word:
My mind churn'd round like murlin' stanes
And a cauld sough gaed thru my banes.
Mair snell it blew and riv'd awa
The haar afore my e'en; but a'
That erlish gairthen had gaen by
And in a lanely place was I;
Whaur naething sounded but the whins
Clawn up to gansh the wheeplin' win's.
I glour'd a' round like ane afaird
O' his ain schedaw; nocht I heard
Till richt afore my e'en upstüde
A harnest body bleach'd o' bluid:

---

spatrels: musical notes; **howff**: dwelling; **souff**: unsound sleep;
styme: spark; **con**: tell; **erlish**: unearthly;

I kent, or he had spak a word,
This deid man wi' the muckle sword.
Liftin' his airm he swung it roun'
And I cud see that on a croun
O' a bare hill I'd taen my stand
Wi' a like hill on ilka hand.
'Here are the Eildons:' Wallace said;
Then louted dounward wi' his blade:
'And yonder in the green kirk-shot
Ligg Merlin and the warlock Scot:
And yonder the guid Douglas fand
The marches o' his promised land
Whaur Bruce's hert, gin it cud stound,
Wud wauken Scotland frae her swound.'
He turn'd him then and in a stride
Had taen me round the bare hillside
Whaur derk against the lift upstüde
The Eildon tree: about its wüd
(Deathly as ivy on an aik)
Was wuppit a twa-heided snake.
Bare, bare, the boughs aince bricht as beryl
Whaur sang the mavis and the merle,
And whaur True Thomas' fairy feir
Won him away for seven year:
Ah! cud he busk his banes, and dree
Yon burn o' bluid, this dowie tree
Wud flichter wi' braw fullyery.
But noo the nicht was comin' owre;
The lither lift began to lour;
As yont the hill the floichans flew
Mair snell the yammerin' blufferts blew;
Nae bleat was there o' beast or bird:
I wud hae spak but had nae word.

---

stound: heavy blow; **swound**: swoon; **busk**: dress;
dowie: spiritless; **lither lift**: gloomy sky; **lour**: threatening rain;
floichans: snowflakes; **snell**: keen; **yammerin'**: complaining;
blufferts: blasts of wind;

The Wallace stüde like he was stane
His cauld lips wordless as my ain,
But saftly on the mirken'd sicht
His muckle blade, wi' an eerie licht,
Glister'd; and in his e'en the poo'r
Low'd up to thraw this weirded hour.
'Twas then I spak: but no my ain
Spirit, in anguishment, alane,
But Scotland's sel, wi' thorter'd pride,
Cried oot upon that cauld hillside:
And her ain name was a' she cried.
Wi' that the Wallace rax't his hicht
Like he wud rive the sternless nicht;
And as his wuntlin' blade cam doun
The snell wind, wi' a wheemerin' soun',
Gaed owre me; and my spirit heard
The challance o' yon singin' word
That whunners like a lowin' sword.
Nae mair nor thrice the Wallace straik;
And first he sklent the heided snake:
He sklent it strauchtly into twa
And kelterin' they skail'd awa;
The ane haud'n southard to his hame,
The ither wast owre Irish faem.
The neist straik, wi' a sklinterin' dird,
Lowden'd the auld tree to the yird
And a' the seepin' sap, like bluid,
Pirr'd saftly frae the cankert wüd:
A sough gaed by me, laich and lang,
Like the owrecome o' an auld-world sang.
The hinmaist straik deep doun was driven
(As it had been a flaucht o' levin)
And riv'd by runt, and craig, until

---

thorter'd: thwarted; **rive**: tear apart; **wuntlin'**: rocking; **sklent**:
sideways; **kelterin'**: swaying; **skail'd**: scattered; **dird**: blow;
flaucht: flash; **levin**: lightning; **runt**: hard, dry stalk; **craig**: cliff;

A muckle slap thraw'd thru the hill
Shawin' the auld tree's wizzen'd rit
A' tangl'd owre that reekin' pit
That gaes richt doun, frae ilka airt,
To the livenin' lowe at the world's hert.
Like ane wha at the deid o' nicht
Is wander'd on a haarie hicht,
And wi' a switherin' breath stands still
Kennin' that at his fit the hill
Hings owre into the mirk o' space,
Sae stüde I be that antrin place.
And first cam up frae oot the pit
A souff; and on the wings o' it
A laich and lanely maunner cam
Like an awaukenin' frae a dwalm:
Sae wunner'd was I and afraid
I kent na a' the sounds I heard
But they were rowth – o' reeshlin' banes,
And sklinterin' rocks, and brakin' chains,
And wails o' women in their thraws,
And the rummlin' march o' harnest raws.
Then maisterin' my mauchless wit
I glour'd richt doun the drumlie pit
And far awa the flichterin' lowe
Gather'd itsel' and, wi' a sough,
Cam loupin'; flaucht on flaucht o' flame
That beller'd owre in fiery faem
And wi' a crack, like the levin's whup,
Flirn'd and flisk'd and fluther'd up.
I wud hae riv'd mysel' awa
But cudna; and the breeshilin' ca'
Jow'd on until its spindrift brunt
The auld tree's wizzen'd rit and runt:

---

haarie: misty; **rowth**: abundant; **thraws**: twists;
harnest: armoured; **raws**: rows;

I goup't upon the glisterin' sicht
My twa e'en blinded wi' the licht
And a' my senses, ane be ane,
Fluff't oot like they had never been;
Yet, far ben in the breist o' me,
I heard the soundin o' the sea.

Whan I cam roun' the lowe was gaen
And I was standin' a' alane;
But whaur the slap had gaunted wide
And whaur, abüne the bare hillside,
The auld tree crin'd; deep in the yird
Wallace had sheuch'd his muckle sword.
And noo the yirlich steer was düne
And up the lowdenin' life the müne
Cam saftly till her cannie licht
Kyth'd on the cauld hill and made bricht.
The caulder sword's begesserant rime
That braidly skinkl'd, styme on styme.
But wha on onie frostit fale
Saw cranreuch bleezin' like a bale,
As in this lifted leam I saw
The hale blade rax itsel' and thraw,
Ryce upon ryce like it had been
A fiery cross a' growin' green
In its ain loupin' leure o' wud;
Till deein' doun – a thistle stüde
Whaur aince had dwin'd the Eildon tree.
There was nae soun': it seem'd to me
On that bare hill nae soun' wud be
For evermair; nor birth, nor death,
As God were haudin' in His breath:
The müne, far in the midmaist lift,

---

slap: passage; **crin'd**: shrank; **yirlich**: wild; **steer**: commotion;
lowdenin': quietening; **kyth'd**: appeared; **begesserant**: sparkling;
styme: particle; **fale**: stretch of grass; **cranreuch**: hoar frost;
bale: bonfire; **leam**: shine;

Ligg'd like a stane nae hand cud shift,
And strauchtly on the thistle's croun
Its lipper licht cam spinnerin' doun.
But a' that stillness, in a crack,
Was by and düne whan at my back
I heard a fitterin' fit; and turn'd
And saw a man wha's twa e'en burn'd
Wi' byspale glamer like he sklent
On routhie years time yet maun tent.
Word-drucken was he, but his words
As the rambusteous lilt o' birds
Wauken'd the thistle; and for lang
I harkint while he sang his sang:
But wi' his words I winna mell
Sin he has screed them a' himsel'.*
Aye richt owreheid the müne ligg'd still
And lows'd her cauld licht on the hill;
But noo she was nae mair alane,
In the lirk o' the lift, for ane be ane
The sma' sternes soom'd frae oot the slack
O' space that gaed awa far back
Ahint the müne; and as they cam
The müne hersel' dreng'd frae her dwalm
And cannily began to steer
Yont her lang nicht o' seven year.
Wi' that the drunken man upstüde
And shog'd the muckle thistle's wüd
Until the flounrie draff like snaw
Flew up, and owre, and far awa:
And weel I kent, as it gaed by,
That on a guidly hill was I;
And that there breer'd, at ilka hand,
The braid shires o' a promised land.
Noo, as the day began to daw,

---

leure: blaze; **byspale**: marvellous; **glamer**: glamour;
routhie: abundant; **tent**: notice; **flounrie**: downy; **draff**: seed;
breer'd: sprouted;

The thistle wi' a warstlin' thraw
Rax't out its airms – and was a tree
Younglin' and green wi' fullyery;
And as the licht low'd in its hert
The flichterin' birds, frae ilka airt,
Cam hameart to their norlan nest
In the saft bieldin o' its breist.
Richt in the rowsan sin the wüd
O' this green tree sae leamin' stüde
Like it had been a buss o' fire;
And as it stüde the warblin' choir
O' birds were singin' o' their hame:
But what they sang I canna name
Though I was singin' wi' the birds
In my ain countrie's lawland words
Lang, lang, I stüde upon that hicht
And aye it was in louthe o' licht;
And aye the birds sang owre their sang;
And aye the growthy tree outflang
Its fullyery afore the sin:
'Daw on o' day that winna düne:'
I sang: *'or Scotland stands abüne*
Her ain deid sel'; and sterkly steers
Into the bairn-time o' her years.'

I wauken'd; and my hert was licht
(Though owre my ain hill cam the nicht)
For aye yon antrin hill I saw
Wi' its green tree in the gowdan daw:
And, as I swaver'd doun the slack,
I heard, aye branglant at my back,
The challance o' the singin' word
That whunners like a lowin' sword.

---

hameart: homeward; **rowsan**: blazing; **leamin'**: shining;
buss: bush; **louthe**: abundance; **swaver'd**: walked feebly;
slack: hollow between hills; **branglant**: ringing, resounding

Birthday

There were three men o' Scotland
Wha rade intill the nicht
Wi' nae müne lifted owre their crouns
Nor onie stern for licht:

Nane but the herryin' houlet,
The broun mouse, and the taed,
Kent whan their horses clapper'd by
And whatna road they rade.

Nae man spak to his brither,
Nor ruggit at the rein;
But drave straucht on owre burn and brae
Or half the nicht was gaen.

Nae man spak to this brither,
Nor lat his hand draw in;
But drave straucht on owre ford and fell
Or nicht was nealy düne.

There cam a flaucht o' levin
That brocht nae thunner ca'
But left ahint a lanely lowe
That wudna gang awa.

---

stern: star; **herryin'**: plundering; **houlet**: owl; **taed**: toad;
ruggit: pulled; **howes**: hollows; **flaucht o' levin**: flash of
lightning; **lowe**: glow;

And richt afore the horsemen,
Whaur grumly nicht had been,
Stüde a' the Grampian Mountains
Wi' the dark howes atween.

Up craigie cleuch and corrie
They rade wi' stany soun',
And saftly thru the lichted mirk
The switherin' snaw cam doun.

They gaed by birk and rowan,
They gaed by pine and fir;
Aye on they gaed or nocht but snaw
And the roch whin was there.

Nae man brac'd back the bridle
Yet ilka fit stüde still
As thru the flichterin' floichan-drift
A beast cam doun the hill.

It steppit like a stallion,
Wha's heid hauds up a horn,
And weel the men o' Scotland kent
It was the unicorn.

It steppit like a stallion,
Snaw-white and siller-bricht,
And on its back there was a bairn
Wha low'd in his ain licht.

---

grumly: grim; **craigie**: rocky; **cleuch**: precipice; **corrie**:
mountain hollow; **birk**: birch; **floichan-drift**: falling snow;

And baith gaed by richt glegly
As day was at the daw;
And glisterin' owre hicht and howe
They saftly smool'd awa.

Nae man but socht his brither
And look't him in the e'en,
And sware that he wud gang a' gates
To cry what he had seen.

There were three men o' Scotland
A' frazit and forforn;
But on the Grampian Mountains
They saw the unicorn.

---

glegly: smoothly; **smool'd awa**: faded, disappeared;
gang a' gates: go everywhere; **frazit and forforn**: amazed
and exhausted

The Thistle Looks at the Drunk Man

The wild November blasts had set
Auld locks lood-tirlin at the yett,
An' brocht the haur, baith cauld an' wet,
Doon fae the North;
Roosin the sea until its ket
Had fleesh'd the Forth.

Nae time wis it for man nor beast
Tae lave the biggin o' their nest;
The cosy hole or chimley-breest
What gien them shelter,
Against the cruel, bitin' East
An' North's weet skelter.

On sic a nicht intae the neuk
I got deep plankit wi' a buik;
Peitry I thocht it by the look
O' lines askewie:
A' wrocht be ane, wi' scribbler's yeuk,
They ca' Wee Hughie.*

I stecher'd on a page or twa
But süne my heid began tae fa;
My braith gaed wi' a soochin ca'
Or wi' a wheep;
An' howdlin owre ayont the wa'
I drapp'd asleep.

---

lood-tirlin': loud-sounding; **ket**: fleece; **fleesh'd**: fleeced;
yeuk: urge; **stecher'd**: laboured;

A Drunk Man Looks at the Thistle Hugh McDiarmid

Monie a dream's been dern'd intill
The heids o' men; an' he's a füle,
They say, wha kerries fae this mull
Tae them ootby:
But Keats tauld o' his lanely hull
An' sae wull I.

I saw a thustle a' alane
Fu' heich abüne the tapmaist Ben;
Onlie ae fit had stotterin gaen
Asklent its sicht,
Whan fou the müne wis, wi' but ane
O' the sterns for licht.

Its heid wis boo'd, in sair africht
Its jabs sae reestit that ye micht
Hae thocht the Deil's ain brinstane licht
Had low'd abüne.
'Thustle!' said I, 'what kind o' plicht
Is this yer in?'

Wi' that it lufted up itsel'
An' wagg'd an airm, an' lat the snell
Blaw o' the mountain rin tae mell
Aboot its body;
Then lauchin' said: 'E'en fowk in Hell
Wud scorn yon toddy!

'But freen, ye'll no ken weel, I wot,
The mark my wurds are drivin' at;
An' juist tae lat ye hear what's what
Come, sit ye doon;
Richt there whaur my drunk neibor sat
Aneath the müne.

---

reestit: down-cast;

'A lad o' pairts he wis; an' brose
Ocht tae hae buskt, abüne his nose,
Ooor couthie genius; till in prose
Or rantin rhyme,
He micht hae heis'd, mair than Montrose,
Ayont a' time.

'But hamely fare wis no for him:
He laidl'd owre his gusty rim
A' kinds o' meat tae stap each whim
Kitlin his void:
Rocher an' Blok an' Joyce (Nim! Nim!!)
Mallarmé, Freud.

'Wi' booze o' a' guffs he wud droon
That honest Doric, as a loon,
He throve on in a bonnie Toun
Whaur fowk still speak
Nae hash o' German, Slav, Walloon
An' bastard Greek.

'Nae doot he thocht his reekin braith
Wud be aboot me as a graith
O' livin water: but Guid faith!
It wis a splore
That brocht me hantle nearer daith
Than ocht afore.

'Whan Wull Dunbar an' Henrysoun
Aft gard me loup tae monie a tune,
Makin' my jeints gang up an' doon
Wi' unco styne;
I kent sma hairm then, bein' a loon;
But that's lang syne.

___

brose: overfed; **buskt**: prepared; **heis'd**: lifted up; **rim**: skin;
graith: wealth; **splore**: frolic; **hantle**: a fair number;
styne: sparkle;

An' gin my boo'd rits hae the spavie
Fu' weel I ken yon loon's purgavie
Is no the yin
Tae make me whustle like a mavie
An' dance tae the tüne.

'Wi' ploys like yon intill my nottle
Or lang I'd süne be düne an' dottle;
Nae penny wheep or spleutrie bottle
Sall straught this back.
Fegs! if it's drams – there's Aristotle
Wi' phiz tae tak.

'Hughie! nae doot ye think 'am waggin
My heid owre lang at ye, an' naggin:
But it's my naitur tae be jaggin
Baith freen an' fae:
Nemo impune (ye ken the taggin)
Lacessit me.'

Wi' that a wind cam up the howes
An' loupit owre the tapmaist knowes,
Flightin' the thustle tae lat louse
A sang o' glee;
Until the lauchter in his boughs
Upwaukin'd me.

---

spavie: spavin; **purgavie**: provision; **nottle**: noddle;
penny wheep: weak beer; **spleutrie**: weak and watery;
fegs:truly; **phiz**: medicine

The Hungry Toun

Torven is a hungry toun,
Whaur the cauld winds blaw,
Aye sotterin wi' weet
Or sotterin wi' snaw.

The cordiner has nae shüne;
The baxter nae bread;
The delver in the bur'al-hole
Maks the brawest bed.

The gavel-ends hing a' agee
And dreep in a' weathers:
The kimmers hinna onie briests,
And the birds nae feathers.

Scrogs and scrunts are on the braes,
Yattle in the yairds;
And wizzent bairns like auld men
Wha hinna onie beards.

---

cordiner: shoemaker; **baxter**: baker; **delver**: gravedigger;
gavle: gable; **agee**: awry; **kimmers**: gossips; **scrogs and
scrunts**: stunted and shrivelled plants; **yattle**: chatter;
wizzent: withered

Day-Dream

Doun be the dark schaw an ootlin-body sat
Wi' a drouth but no a droggle;
The weet dreep-drappin on the auld farrant hat
He had taen frae a tattie-bogle.

The bairn that he was cam rinnin yon wey
Whaur there wasna onie wey afore him:
And the wonders o' the world gaed raikin by
Whaur there wasna onie day attour them.

Ae Simmer's Day

Up by the caller fountain
A' through a simmer's day,
I heard the gowk gang cryin
Abüne the ferny brae.

The reemlin licht afore me
Gaed up; the wind stüde still:
Only the gowk's saft whistle
Lowden'd alang the hill.

The wee burn loppert laichly;
A bird cam and was gaen:
I keekit round ahint me
For I was a' my lane.

---

ootlin-body: stranger; **droggle**: drink; **tattie-bogle**:
scarecrow; **raikin'**: ranging; **gowk**: cuckoo; **caller**: fresh;
reemlin': shimmering; **loppert**: rippled; **laichly**: lowly

Lauch Whan Ye Can

'Lauch whan ye can,'
Said the puddock to the taed:
'For the fairest days are flichty,
And we're a lang while dead.'

'Hey!' sech'd the taed,
Wi' a waggle o' his pow:
'I've juist buried my guid-brither
And I'm gey wae the noo.'

'Come awa, man,
Fash nae mair for what has been:
Lat's mak merry wi' the livin
Sae lang's our luck is in.'

Juist as he spak
He was trod on be a coo.
'May the Lord forgie me, puddock,
I'm lauchin herty noo.'

Hal o' the Wynd

Hal o' the Wynd he taen the field
Alang be the skinklin Tay:
And he hackit doun the men o' Chattan;
Or was it the men o' Kay?

When a' was owre he dichted his blade
And steppit awa richt douce
To draik his drouth in the Skinners' Vennel
At clapperin Clemmy's house.

Hal o' the Wynd had monie a bairn;
And bairns' bairns galore
Wha wud speer about the bluidy battle
And what it was fochten for.

'Guid-faith! my dawties, I never kent;
But yon was a dirlin day
Whan I hackit doun the men o' Chattan;
Or was it the men o' Kay?'

The Secret

The grave-stanes at Kinclaven Kirk
Are cantl'd a' agee;
And wha staigs by in the pit-mirk
May hear what he canna see.

And it winna be the puddock's croak,
Nor the burn that saftly drools,
But the singin o' the corpie-folk
Maunnerin up frae the mools.

And it winna be at the midnicht hour,
But whan the grey is near,
That yon lilt that was sae laich afore
Will be soundin licht and clear.

There is but ane in Kinclaven toun
Wha kens what he daurna tell;
And he has the face o' a leerie loon
Aye lauchin to himsel'.

---

cantl'd: tilted; **agee**: awry; **staigs**: walks, stalks;
pit-mirk: deep darkness; **leerie**: shining (lamplighter);
corpie-folk: dead folk; **maunnerin'**: mumbling;
mools: fine soil

Far Awa in Araby

Far awa in Araby,
Whaur the first world had been,
Sae growthy frae its wilderness
A tree lifts a' alane.

Siller in the licht o' the müne,
Gowd in the licht o' day;
Amang its fleurs a fiery bird
Aye makin melody.

Frae battles that were focht lang syne
A rummlin wind comes owre;
And kings wi' gauntin faces rive
On through the switherin stour.

A brichtness glimmers frae their banes,
And frae their stany e'en,
Siller in the licht o' the day,
Gowd in the licht o' the müne.

Aye in the scarrow o' the tree
The flitterin fleurs dounfa';
And nidder into naethingness
Afore they licht ablow.

The lovers wha hae martyr'd love,
And will nae mair be blest,
Here in their restlessness maun rove
And canna come on rest:

Ayont their dead and hungry hands
The fa'in fleurs drift by;
Siller in the licht o' the müne,
Gowd in the licht o' day.

---

growthy: well-grown; **scarrow**: shadow; **nidder**: shrivel

The Gowdan Ba'

The muckle müne noo rows attowre
The humphie-backit brae;
And skimmers doun the Carse o' Gower
And the fluther o' the Tay.

O earth, ye've tin'd your gowdan ba';
And yonder, in the nicht,
It birls clean on and far awa
Sae wee and siller-bricht.

Roch Winter

Roch-handed winter has wauken'd up
And is rowtin doun the glens:
He taks the trees in his course grup
And rattles a' their banes.

Birds flee awa; and frichten'd baes
Creep into corner and hole:
The earth itsel' gangs white in the face
To hear yon wild man yowl.

---

rows: rolls; **attowre**: across; **humphie-backit**: hump-backed;
skimmers: shimmers; **fluthers**: rushes; **tin'd**: lost;
siller-bricht: silver-bright; **rowtin'**: roaring

The Wind

A blind and hameless body
Round-by the mirklin hour
Cam chappin on the winnock
And fummlin at the door.

Back and fore he fitter'd
Sae wander'd and alane;
But ilka lock was sneckit,
And nane wud lat him in.

Syne wi' a breengin belloch
His rousin rage brak lowse,
And the dingin o' his dirdums
Rattl'd a' the house.

The Daft Tree

A tree's a leerie kind o' loon,
Weel happit in his emerant goun
Through the saft simmer days:
But, fegs, whan baes are in the fauld,
And birds are chitterin wi' the cauld,
He coosts aff a' his claes.

---

breengin: impetuous; **belloch**: bellow; **dirdrums**: great
noise; **leerie**: shining, glowing; **happit**: happy;
simmer: summer; **fegs**: goodness; **whan**: when; **baes**: sheep;
coosts: casts; **claes**: clothes

The Lanely Müne

Saftly, saftly, through the mirk
The müne walks a' hersel':
Ayont the brae; abüne the kirk;
And owre the dunnlin bell.
I wudna be the müne at nicht
For a' her gowd and a' her licht.

Bawsy Broon

Dinna gang out the nicht:
Dinna gang out the nicht:
Laich was the müne as I cam owre the muir;
Laich was the lauchin though nane was there:
Somebody nippit me,
Somebody trippit me;
Somebody grippit me roun' and aroun':
I ken it was Bawsy Broon:
I'm shair it was Bawsy Broon.

Dinna win out the nicht:
Dinna win out the nicht:
A rottan reeshl'd as I ran be the sike,
And the dead-bell dunnl'd owre the auld kirk-dyke:
Somebody nippit me,
Somebody trippit me;
Somebody grippit me roun' and aroun':
I ken it was Bawsy Broon:
I'm shair it was Bawsy Broon.

---

dinna: don't; laich: low; lauchin': laughing; win: get out,
escape; rottan: rat; reeshl'd: rustled; syke: small stream;
dunnl'd: rang; kirk-dyke: church wall

In the Nicht

Yon's the queer hour whan a' be yoursel'
Ye wauken in the mirk;
And far awa ye can hear the bell
Dinnle abüne the kirk.

Yon's the queer hour whan the fittery clock
Comes knappin alang the wa';
And your hert begins to knockity-knock,
And your breath canna ca'.

Yon's the queer hour whan the murlin mouse
Charks on and is never düne;
And the wind is wheemerin round the house:
Lat me in, lat me in!

The Thistle

Blaw, wind, blaw
The thistle's head awa:
For ilka head ye whup in the air
The yird will lift a hunner, or mair,
Doun in the lair o' yon sheuch be the schaw.

---

whup: whip; **yird**: garden; **lair**: mud; **sheuch**: trench;
schaw: little wood

Coorie in the Corner

Coorie in the corner, sitting a' alane,
Whan the nicht wind's chappin
On the winnock-pane:
Corrie in the corner, dinna greet ava;
It's juist a wee bit goloch
Rinning up the wa'.

Wintry Nicht

What dae ye think I saw last nicht
Whan the müne cam owre Kinnoull?
A puddock, wi' a cannel-licht,
Wha socht his puddock-stool.

The wintry wind gluff't oot his glim
And skirl'd ahint a sauch:
The chitterin' schedows loup't at him;
The müne shog'd wi' a lauch.

Doun be a dyke he grat alane;
Puir baest, sae made a mock:
The frostit draps dirl'd, ane be ane,
Upon the frostit rock.

---

coorie: cower; **winnock**: window; **goloch**: insect;
puddock: frog; **socht**: sought; **gluff't**: blew; **glim**: gleam;
skirl'd: screamed; **sauch**: willow; **schedows**: shadows;
shog: shook; **dirl'd**: struck

Bed-Time

Cuddle-doun, my bairnie;
The dargie day is düne:
Yon's a siller sternie
Ablow the siller müne:

Like a wabster body
Hingin on a threed,
Far abüne my laddie
And his wee creepie-bed.

Compensation

Stumpy Dunn, like a fell lot mair
Wha straid awa sae trig,
Has traikit hame again frae the war
Wi' a medal and a lang pin-leg.

Up wi' your gless for Stumpy Dunn
And lat there be nae stint;
We're no owre shair o' what he has won
But we're shair o' what he has tint.

Monie a swankie, wha aince was here
And swackit aff his swig,
Wud think it weel to be hame frae the war
Wi' a medal and a lang pin-leg.

---

dargie: busy; **wabster**: spider; **trig**: neat; **stint**: shortcomings;
tint: lost; **swankie**: strapping young fellow; **swackit**: drank

The Sailor-Man

'What hae ye düne?' the auld-wife dar'd,
As the sailor-man straik'd by:
But he staig'd straucht on like he hadna heard
And wi' never a hint her wey.

'Whaur hae ye been?' the jillet fleer'd,
As the sailor-man haik'd by:
But he breisted on like he hadna heard
And wi' never a glint her wey.

'Wha hae ye seen?' the wee bairn speer'd,
As the sailor-man rak'd by:
'O! I hae seen a grey-beast wi' a beard
Wha runches rocks like hey.'

The Brig

Amang the skinklin stanners
In the cannie simmer days
Our brig wides through the rinnles
That lapper owre his taes:

But whan the weet winds bluster,
And tattery are the trees,
He warsles in roch water
That gurls abüne his knees.

---

dar'd: dared; **straik'd**: strode; **staig'd**: stalked; **straucht**: straight;
jillet: flighty girl; **fleer'd**: mocked; **haiked**: travelled; **breisted**:
breasted; **speer'd**: asked; **runches**: crunches; **rinnles**: stream;
skinkling stanners: shining small stones

The Wind

Wha wudna be me?
I caper and flee
And hae nae care for oniebody.
I rugg the forest be the hair:
I swell the water abüne the rock:
I shog the steeple, and make a mock
O turret and too'r:
Castle-wa's trummle whan I lowp owre.

Wha wudna be me?
I caper and flee
And hae nae care for oniebody.
Am I no the wind;
Sae fliskie and free;
Sae soupple and swack?
But alack, and alack,
I am blind:
I am blind.

Black Day

A skelp frae his teacher
For a' he cudna spell:
A skelp frae his mither
For cowpin owre the kail.

A skelp frae his brither
For clourin his braw bat:
And a skelp frae his faither
For the Lord kens what.

---

kail: broth; **clourin**: hitting

Reverie

The garden, like a day-dream, now invites me
To share its sunny hours;
Till one by one my thoughts, unwittingly,
Wing forth from the blood's edge;
More free than the birds they pass,
Bird-like, beyond the flowers
To step on grass which smoothly meets the hedge.
They have become a part of the coloured earth;
And yet the eyes which see no longer see
Flower, or grass, or tree:
The world is shrunk into a little garth
And life to phantasy.
A petal falls; a wind shoulders the bough;
A chattering bird beyond the garden flies?
Is it the selfsame day? I would avow
The grass is greener now;
More blue the skies:
With this awakening what dream-world dies?

Song

The leaf drifts from the tree:
The iron image slowly rots away:
Rocks from their roots dissolve into the sea;
And stars, which blinded, dwindled from their day.

There is no sorrow here:
No bitterness in the momentary throng;
Which hurries on like birds out of the year:
Their music dies but endless is the song.

Heart, that has learned to bless
The falling leaf, the fated butterfly,
Seek not to hoard even your happiness
From the indifferent worm, the indifferent sky.

The Mood

Wearied by common intercourse I stare,
Beyond this murmurous room, grown unaware
Of all the frothy words which flow, in a flood,
Over my head: the mind drowned deep
Answers in ayes and noes as if asleep:
But deeper than the intellectual reach
Of wordy speech my hearkening blood
Hears, from a neighbouring wood,
The cuckoo's cry.

I listen, and a man that is not I
Listens; our kindred sense now gone
Back to an age of stone:
And back, and back, until with dumb accord
We understand the cuckoo's wordless word;
Which, in a moment shattering space and time
Upon a rhyme,
Bids us accept the wisdom of this moon
And recognise, in silence, our own solitude.

To the Future

He, the unborn, shall bring
From blood and brain
Songs that a child can sing
And common men:

Songs that the heart can share
And understand;
Simple as berries are
Within the hand:

Such a sure simpleness
As strength may have;
Sunlight upon the grass:
The curve of the wave.

In Time of Tumult

The thunder and the dark
Dwindle and disappear:
The free song of the lark
Tumbles in air.

The froth of the wave-drag
Falls back from the pool:
Sheer out of the crag
Lifts the white gull.

Heart! keep your silence still
Mocking the tyrant's mock:
Thunder is on the hill;
Foam on the rock.

The Unknown

There is a shape of humankind
Still to be recognised;
A murdered man who haunts the mind
And is not exorcised.

From every battlefield he comes
In silent nakedness:
And he outlives the muffled drums,
The oblivion of grass.

He has no name; no seal of birth;
No sign of saint or slave:
He is a man of common earth
Born from a common grave.

Bone of our bone: blood of our blood:
Our freedom and our fate:
His sires raged in the savage wood,
And still his brothers hate.

His heritage is in his hands;
And in the light and air;
And in the earth whereon he stands;
For he is everywhere.

And yet he walks his native ground
An alien without rest,
Bearing Cain's curse and Abel's wound
Upon his flesh confessed:

Blood of our blood: bone of our bone:
Brother since time began:
Look on his anguish nor disown
That he is everyman.

Song

End is in beginning;
And in beginning end:
Death is not loss, nor life winning;
But each and to each is friend.

The hands which give are taking;
And the hands which take bestow:
Always the bough is breaking
Heavy with fruit or snow.

Jamie

Yonder is the knowe; and whan thistles are upon it
Auld Jamie stands there wi' fleurs for a bonnet.

Jamie has a cronie; Jamie has three –
The laverock, the corbie, and the sma' hinny-bee.

The laverock trocks wi' heaven, the corbie wi' hell;
The hinny-bee flees on atween and disna fash itsel'.

Jamie whistled at the plew; Jamie won his queyn;
Jamie was a strappan lad – but that was lang-syne.

---

trocks: keeps busy with; **fash**: bother

The Gowk

Ayont the linn; ayont the linn,
Whaur gowdan wags the gorse,
A gowk gaed cryin': 'Come ye in:
I've fairins in my purse.'

'My bield is o' the diamond stane
Wi' emerant atween:
My bonnie een are yours alane,
An' rubies are my een.'

My faither brak a sauchy stick;
My mither wal'd a stane:
An' weel I set it for the trick
Tae mak the gowk my ain.

The stane was set; the shot was shot;
The flichterin' burd was fund:
But nocht aboot that lanely spot
O' gowd or diamond.

It had nae siller for a croun;
Nae rubies for its een:
But a' the crammasy ran doun
Whaur aince its breist had been.

I look't; an' there was nane tae see
The fairin I had taen:
I hung it on a roden-tree
An' left it a' alane.

---

linn: waterfall; **wags**: waves; **fairins**: presents; **bield**: shelter;
sauchy: willow; **crammasy**: crimson; **roden-tree**: rowan tree

Fear

Aince in the mornin' early,
The mornin' o' the year,
I dug deep doun intill the yird
And happit a' my fear.

I happit owre my fractious fear
And cried: 'Lie laich ye füle:'
But whan aince mair I gaed that gate
I heard the leaves o' dule.

I heard the chunnerin' leaves o' dule
And wudna bide to hear:
But whan aince mair I gaed that gate
I saw the fruct o' fear.

I saw the heavy fruct o' fear
Sae mindfu' o' my youth:
And raxin' up a desolate hand
I gether'd in my ruth.

---

dule: sorrow; **fruct**: fruit

Impromtu on the Quite Impossible She

This is the kind o' wife I wud wed
Though I dout she'll no be in my bed:
Better owre strappan nor owre sma':
Better owre steerie nor owre slaw:
Better owre youthie nor owre auld:
Better owre couthie nor owre cauld:
Better owre easy nor owre strack:
Better owre snoddit nor owre slack:
Better owre breistit nor owre spare:
Better owre swarthy nor owre fair:
Better owre gabless nor owre gash:
Better owre rogie nor owre lash:
Better owre hameart nor owre gaun:
Better owre tenty nor owre blaw'n:
Better owre merry nor owre mimp:
Better owre loavish nor owre skrimp:
Better owre dawtie nor owre dour:
Better owre sautie nor owre sour:
This is the kind o' wife I wud wed
Though I dout she'll no be in my bed.

---

steerie: bustling; **strack**: measured; **gabless**: no talk;
gash: talkative; **rogie**: roguish; **lash**: lazy; **hameart**:
homeward; **tenty**: careful; **mimp**: prim; **loavish**: generous;
dawtie: darling; **dour**: miserable; **sautie**: salty

Dream

Out o' the glimmerin darkness walk'd the shade,
Walk't on atween the planets and the stars
As in a münelicht yirden fu' o' fleurs.
Quietly he gaed and wi' a quiet hand
Lifted the glintin earth and cried on Man
Attowre the darkness; and the human shape
Cam to the shade, and stüde, and spak nae word.
Syne, as the sound o' silence, the shade spak:
'Here is the earth I gie ye, like a rose,
To be the hairst and death o' your desire.'
But Man stüde still; and cried wi' angry voice:
'There is nae fareweel to desire; and nane
Can gether joy and sorrow like a fleur.'
And at the word the shade turn'd and was gaen
Back to the blackness: but the human shape
That kent nae end to gledness and to grief
Boo'd owre the earth as it had been a bairn.

Yellow Yorlins

Three yorlins flitter'd frae the elder tree;
Three glisterin yorlins gledsome on the e'e:
Pity the blind folk, wha hae never seen
The yellow yorlin, for they canna ken
Sae sma' a sicht is a' a man need hae
To keep his hert abüne its misery.

---

yorlins: yellow-hammer; **boo'd**: bowed

Sic a Hoast

Sic a hoast hae I got:
Sic I hoast hae I got:
I dout my days are on the trot;
Sic a hoast hae I got.

Whauzlin like an auld tup,
I grup whatever's there to grup
And clocher half my stummick up;
Sic a hoast hae I got.

Physic, poultices, and pills,
Reekin rousers, reemin yills,
Nane can shift this hell o' ills;
Sic a hoast hae I got.

The delver at his deathly trade
Gies a rattle wi' his spade;
Blinks an e'e, and shakes his head;
Sic a hoast hae I got.

Sic a hoast hae I got:
Sic a hoast hae I got:
I dout my days are on the trot;
Sic a hoast hae I got.

---

whauzlin: wheezing; **tup**: ram; **grup**: grasp; **clocher**: cough;
reekin' rousers: smelly medicines; **reemin yills**: steaming
toddies

The Buckie Braes

It isna far frae our toun
Be onie gait that gaes;
It isna far frae our toun
To gang to the Buckie Braes;
Whaur the wee linn lowps the craigies
And whaur the cushats croun;
And the happers in the growthy grass
Are diddlin owre their tune;
Wi' a chickie-chick-chickerie,
Dickie-dick-dickerie,
Tickie-tick-tickerie,
Jiggety-jig.

Monie a bairn frae our toun
In the canty simmer days;
Monie a bairn frae our toun
Haiks up to the Buckie Braes,
Whaur the birk links in wi' the rodden
And the burnie rinnles doun;
And the happers in the growthy grass
Are diddlin owre their tune;
Wi' a chickie-chick-chickerie,
Dickie-dick-dickerie,
Tickie-tick-tickerie,
Jiggety-jig.

---

be ony gait: by any road; **linn**: waterfall; **cushats**: wood-
pigeons; **rodden**: rowan; **happers**: grasshoppers

An Alphabet for Caledonian Bairns

A for an aik,
B for a bake,
C for a corbie-craw ca'in craik! craik!
D for a doo,
E for a ewe,
F for a flitter-mouse fleein flichtfu'.
G for a gook,
H for a heuk,
I for an ill-wind in the ingle neuk.
J for a jay,
K for a kay,
L for a lang-legg't loon lampin owre the lay.
M maks a maen,
N never nane,
O cries ochonerie, ochone and ochaine!
P for a pack,
Q for a quack,
R for a rodden-deer rowtin on a rock.
S for a sporran,
T for a thorn,
U for that unco beast our ain unicorn.
V for a virl,
W for a whirl,
Y for the yarie and yanky yellow-yorl.

---

aik: oak; **doo**: dove; **gook**: gowk, cuckoo; **heauk**: sicle; **ingle**: fireside; **neuk**: corner; **kay**: jackdaw; **lay**: lea; **maen**: moan; **ochonerie, etc.**: expressions of sorrow; **rowtin**: roaring; **virl**: ferrule; **yarie**: alert; **yanky**: active; **yorl**: yellow-hammer

The Wish

Doun in the dark a worm thocht lang
Hoo braw it wud be to sing:
For there's far mair hert'nin in a sang
Nor in onie ither thing.

A mavie wha was takin a turn
Cam by and cockit his pow
To hear the bit cratur sech and girn
Doun there in its hidie-howe.

'I maun dae my best for this puir wee smout,'
Lauch't the mavie to himsel':
'He'll mak a braw sang wud he but come oot –
And learn hoo to flee as weel.'

---

pow: head; **sech**: sigh; **girn**: complain

The Hungry Mauchs

There was a moupit, mither mauch
Wha hadna onie meat;
And a' her bairns, aye gleg to lauch,
Were gather'd round to greet.

'O mither, mither, wha was yon
That breisted on through bluid:
Wha crackit crouns, and wrackit touns,
And was our faither's pride?

'O mither, mither, wha was yon
That was sae frack and fell?'
'My loves, it was Napoleon
But he's sma' brok himsel'.'

'Noo lat us a' lowt on our knees,'
The spunkiest shaver said:
'And prig upon the Lord to gie's
Napoleon frae the dead.'

The mither mauch began to lauch:
'Ye needna fash nor wurn:
He's clappit doun, and happit roun',
And in a kist o' airn.'

---

mauchs: maggots; **moupit**: drooping; **gleg**: quick; **frack**:
bold; **fell**: extreme; **brok**: fragments; **lowt**: bow low;
spunkiest: liveliest; **prig**: plead; **wurn**: complain; **airn**: iron;

'O whaur, O whaur's my faither gaen?'
The peeriest bairn outspak.
'Wheesht, wheesht, ye wee bit looniekin,
He'll fetch a ferlie back.'

'Will he bring hame Napoleon's head
To cockle up my kite?'
'He'll bring ye hame the wuff o' bluid
That's reid and rinnin yet.'

---

peeriest: smallest; **looniekin**: wee fellow; **ferlie**: wonder;
cockle up my kite: warm up my stomach

Time and Space

Wi' a' thing steady on the grund,
Whan even grass-blades dinna steer,
The thocht o' the hale world whurlin round
Is byordinary queer.

And it disna seem a droller thocht –
That a' man's mercies and mishaps
Gang by a licht as a levin-flaucht
Atween twa thunder-claps.

The Hunt

Yon stag breists owre the haary hicht
And westers be a lanely wey:
His gowdan horns wi' glitterin licht
Brund on the world as he branks by.

And aye the hunter raiks ahint:
And aye the hunt is never düne:
The white horse glintin, and the glint
O' thranging dugs wi' stany e'en.

---

brund: flashes; **branks**: holds head high; **raikes**: ranges

The Herryin o' Jenny Wren

Jenny Wren's wee eggs are awa;
Sic a t'dae and hullie-balloo:
She deav'd the mavie and the craw,
The laverock and the cushie-doo.

She toddl'd here, she toddl'd there;
She gar'd the cock craw at her biddin:
And a' the day, or his hawse gat sair,
He was her bell-man round the midden.

Then up and spak a clockin-hen:
'Hoo monie eggs are taen awa?'
'Last nicht I'd six,' sabb'd Jenny Wren,
'And noo I hae nae mair nor twa.'

'It's lang sin I've been at the sküle
And little lare I hae and a';
But,' quod the hen, 'gin I'm nae füle
Fower o' your eggs are taen awa.'

'O wha, wi' mither wit, need fash
For onie mair,' cried Jenny Wren:
'Lat Solomon wauk up and clash
His claivers wi' this clockin-hen.'

---

deav'd: deafened: **gar'd**: caused; **lare**: education;

'Noo, by my troth, sin I'm a mither
I'll name fower reavers,' said the hen:
'The whutterick's ane, the tod's anither,
The rottan, and auld Nickie-ben.'

Then Jennie Wren and a' the birds
Gaed hotterin, owre knock and knowe,
Or they had come to jow their words
At ilka reaver's hidie-howe.

The sleekit tod keek't frae his house
And lowted round to ane and a':
Then sware, as mim as onie mouse,
That he had taen nae eggs awa

The rottan on his hint-legs stüde
And, liftin up twa watery e'en,
Ca'd doun strang curses on his bluid
Gin onie eggs he'd ever taen.

The whutterick, whan he saw the steer,
Lauch't as he sklent alang his snout,
'Shüd I hae seen your eggs, my dear,
I'd taen the hale half-dizzen out.'

Doun in a shog-bog Nickie-ben
Heard the lour chitter o' the birds;
Ans lowpin on a fuggy stane
Said a' his say in twa-three words:

'Gae hame, gae hame, wee Jenny Wren;
It's no for me to name a cronie:
And ca' in on yon clockin-hen
To spear gin twa frae twa leaves onie.'

---

reavers: thieves; **whutterick**: weasel; **tod**: fox; **rottan**: rat;
Nickie-ben: devil; **knock and knowe**: hill and hillock;
jow: sing; **lour**: threatening; **fuggy**: mossy

Daft Sang

Whan doors are steek't, and a' are hame,
It's then I pu' my bauchles on:
Whan folk are beddit wi' their dream
The hale world is my causey-croun.

The hale world is my causey-croun;
The hackit heuch my steppie-stair:
I whistle and the wind comes doun;
And on the wind I gang oniewhaur.

And on the wind I gang oniewhaur,
But nane will ken what I hae seen:
For the world ends – and it isna far;
But nane will ken whaur I hae been.

But nane will ken whaur I hae been
Atween the glimmer and the grey;
Nor hear the clapper o' the müne
Ding up the nicht, ding doun the day.

---

steek't: shut; **bauchles**: old shoes; **causey-croun**: street-crown; **heuch**: cliff

Wintry Moment

Dark the tree stüde
In the snell air:
A rickle o' wüd
Scrunted and bare.

D'ye ken yon hour
(As lane and black)
Whan the hert is dour
And the bluid is brack:

Whan the breist's a door
Shut to the licht:
D'ye ken yon hour
In your ain nicht?

And syne the flird
That cud gar ye greet:
The glisk o' a bird;
A bairn in the weet:

And the livenin' bluid
Gethers its poo'r,
As the sterk wüd
Whan winter's owre.

---

snell: keen; **brack**: brine; **flird**: flutter; **glisk**: glimpse

Hunt the Gowk

What guid has it düne onie ane
Wha has gaen a' roun' the airth –
An' gowpit on the Brahmaputra
An' the ootfa' o' the Congo;
An' kent the graith o' the Amazon
Lang eftir the hinnermaist hicht
Smool'd oot o' sicht – an' cam' aince mair
Tae his bairn-place: an dee'd
Afore he saw hoo bonnily the burn
Gaed by his ain back-door.

A Bairn's Sang

Round and around and a three times three;
Polly and Peg and Pansy:
Round and around the muckle auld tree;
And it's round a' the world whan ye gang wi' me
Round the merry-metanzie:
And it's round a' the world whan ye gang wi' me
Round the merry-metanzie.

The wind blaws loud and the wind blaws hee;
Polly and Peg and Pansy:
Blaw, wind, blaw, as we lilt on the lea;
For it's round a' the world whan ye gang wi' me
Round the merry-metanzie:
For it's round a' the world whan ye gang wi' me
Round the merry-metanzie.

merry-metanzie: jingo ring

Ballad

Far in the nicht whan faint the müne
My love knock't at the door:
He spak nae word as he walkit in,
And wi' nae sound stepp't owre.

White was his face in the thin licht,
And white his hands and feet:
Like snaw, that in itsel is bricht,
White was his windin-sheet.

He look't on me wi' sichtless e'en,
And yet his e'en were kind:
And a' the joys that we had taen
Thrang'd up into my mind.

And for the whilie he was near,
Glimmerin in the gloom,
I thocht the hale o' the world was there
Sae sma' in a sma' room.

---

windin'-sheet: grave cloth

Craigie Knowes

Gin morning daw
I'll hear the craw
On Craigie Knowes
Wauk up the sin:

Wauk up the sin
Wi' caw on caw
Whan day comes in
On Craigie Knowes:

On Craigie Knowes
A' round about
I'll hear the craw
Or day de düne:

Or day be düne
And sterns come out,
And houlets hoot
On Craigie Knowes.

The Fiddler

A fiddler gaed fiddlin through our toun
Wi' bells on his broo and sterns on his shoon;
And the dominie, wabster, souter and miller
Cam out wi' gear and cam out wi' siller.
Ho! Ho! lauch't the fiddler as round him ran
The bairns o' the gaberlunzie-man
Wha sang, as he heistit up his pack –
Tak tent o' the hand that claws your back.

The fiddler he fiddl'd anither tune
As he cam back hame through our toun:
And the dominie, wabster, souter and miller
A' steekit their doors and climpit their siller.
Waes me! cried the fiddler as round him ran
The bairns o' the gaberlunzie-man
Wha sang, as they heistit up his pack –
Tak tent o' the hand that claws your back.

The Muckle Man

There was a muckle man
Wi' a muckle black beard
Wha rade a muckle horse
Through a muckle kirk-yaird:

Hallachin and yallachin
He rattl'd on the stanes:
Hallachin and yallachin
He birl'd abüne the banes:

Up and doun and up and doun
Wi' muckle steer and stour,
Wallopin a muckle whup
Owre and owre and owre.

---

gear: food and drink; **gaberlunzie**: beggar; **tak tent**: take heed

Corbie Sang

The merle in the hauch sings sweet,
The mavie on the hill:
But I mak merry at my meat
And craik to please mysel'.
The licht maun low'r, the sang maun owre,
The grumlie nicht be lang:
Ye canna glowk afore ye howk
Sae lat your straik be strang.

O! bonnie is the simmer sün
And the flourish on the tree:
But the mauchies in a murlie bane
Are bonnier to me.
The wind maun blaw, the fleur maun fa',
The grumlie nicht be lang:
Ye canna glowk afore ye howk
Sae lat your straik be strang.

---

merle: blackbird; **hauch**: low ground; **mavie**: thrush;
craik: croak; **maun**: must; **grumlie**: sullen;
glowk: crow call over carrion; **howk**: pick at: **straik**: strike;
mauchies: maggots; **murlie**: rotting

Gloria Mundi

Though a' the hills were paper
And a' the burns were ink;
Though a man wi' the years o' Ben Voirlich
Wrocht at the crambo-clink;

Getherin the world's glory,
Aye there afore his e'en,
In the day-licht, and the grey-licht,
And the cannel-licht o' the müne;

Lang, lang, or the makin were ended
His rowth o' years were by;
And a' the hills wud be midden-heaps,
And a' the burns dry.

Sang

I wudna be a mowdie
That hiddles frae the licht:
I wudna be a bawkie-bird
That whitters oot at nicht.

I wudna be a houlit
Aye gowkin at the müne:
I wudna be a puddle-doo
That lowps but canna rin:

But I wud be yon gowdan bird
That hings attour the cairn,
Sae far abüne the gallopin deer
And the rory burn.

---

crambo-clink: rhyme; **mowdie**: mole; **bawkie-bird**: bat;
puddle-doo: puddock, frog

Supper

Steepies for the bairnie
Sae moolie in the mou':
Parritch for a strappan lad
To mak his beard grow.

Stovies for a muckle man
To keep him stout and hale:
A noggin for the auld carl
To gar him sleep weel.

Bless the meat, and bless the drink,
And the hand that steers the pat:
And be guid to beggar-bodies
Whan they come to your yett.

---

steepies: bread dipped in milk or water; **parritch**: porridge;
noggin: cup of ale; **carl**: old man; **pat**: pot

Aince Upon A Day

Aince upon a day my mither said to me:
Dinna cleip and dinna rype
And dinna tell a lee.
For gin ye cleip a craw will name ye,
And gin ye rype a daw will shame ye;
And a snail will heeze its hornies out
And hike them round and round about
Gin ye yell a lee.

Aince upon a day, as I walkit a' my lane,
I met a daw, and monie a craw,
And a snail upon a stane.
Up gaed the daw and didna shame me:
Up gaed ilk craw and didna name me:
But the wee snail heez'd its hornies out
And hik'd them round and round about
And – goggl'd at me.

---

cleip: tell tales; **rype**: steal; **gin**: if; **daw**: jackdaw; **heeze**: lift;
hike: swing

The Merry Moment

No muckle in his head
But gledness in his hert,
Habby stots alang the road
Ahint the waterin-cairt.

Bare legs abüne bare feet,
And breeks about his hoch;
Spurtlin up the sprenty weet
That gars him lowp and lauch.

Wha wudna gang this airt
And be a gallus lad –
On ahint a waterin-cairt
Alang the stourie road?

A Scowtherie Day

The weet stanes glint frae the stibbly fields
And the windle-straes blaw by:
The wee beasts hunker into their bields
And nae birds cry.

Frae raggity rungs the fluffers flap;
The flungin burn fraiths doun:
And a drucken cock on the steeple-tap
Gangs yankin roun'.

---

spurtlin': splashing; **hoch**: thigh; **sprenty**: sprinkling;
scowtherie: showery; **windle-straes**: withered grass blade;
rungs: tree branches; **fluffers**: loose leaves; **bields**: shelters

A Laddie's Sang

O! it's owre the braes abüne our toun
Whan the simmer days come in;
Whaur the blue-bells grow, and the burnies row,
And gowdan is the whin.

The gowk sings frae the birken-schaw,
And the laverock far aboon:
The bees bummer by, the peesies cry,
And the lauchin linn lowps doun.

Sang

Hairst the licht o' the müne
To mak a siller goun;
And the gowdan licht o' the sün
To mak a pair o' shoon:

Gether the draps o' dew
To hing about your throat;
And the wab o' the watergaw
To wark yoursel' a coat:

And you will ride oniewhaur
Upon the back o' the wind;
And gang through the open door
In the wa' at the world's end.

---

whin: gorse; **peesies**: plovers; **watergaw**: rainbow

Laverock's Lilt

O! I hae the hert to sing;
And I hae a sang that's clear;
And I hae a whittery wing
To fluff me up in the air:

And wha wudna spirl wi' me
Skimmerin into the blue
And watch the world grow peerie-wee
Sae far awa doun ablow?

Second Childhood

Whan Barrie cam to Paradise
He gar'd the place look droller
Sin they rigg'd him out in velvet breeks
And a braw clean Eton collar.

He skippit about a briar-buss,
And cares he hadna onie,
For the Lord has pity on the bairns
Wha belang to Caledonie.

Her likely lads are wurlin weans,
And cudna be onie ither,
Sin a toom howe is in the breist
O' their sair forjaskit mither.

---

spirl: run about; **peerie-wee**: small; **briar-buss**: briar bush;
wurlin': puny; **toom**: empty; **howe**: hollow;
forjaskit: exhausted

The Greetin Bairnie

Sic a greetin bairnie,
Sic a bruckit face,
Ye maunna be sae girnie
In they bricht, braw days.

Licht is lowpin owre ye;
Gowks lauch frae the wüd;
Fleurs dance on afore ye;
A' the world is gled.

Gin the sün were sumphie
There wud aye be nicht:
Gin the müne were grumphie
There wud be nae licht.

Sic a greetin bairnie,
Sic a bruckit face,
Ye maunna be sae girnie
In they bricht, braw days.

---

bruckit: soiled; **sumphie**: sulky

Ballad

O! shairly ye hae seen my love
Doun whaur the waters wind:
He walks like ane wha fears nae man
And yet his e'en are kind.

O! shairly ye hae seen my love
At the turnin o' the tide;
For then he gethers in the nets
Doun be the waterside.

O! lassie I hae seen your love
At the turnin o' the tide;
And he was wi' the fisher-folk
Doun be the waterside.

The fisher-folk were at their trade
No far frae Walnut Grove;
They gether'd in their dreepin nets
And fund your ain true love.

Balm

Teeny Dott o' Madderty
Was streekit in her kist
Wi' a pickle aipple-ringie
Preen'd on her breist.

It aye had been her comfort
At preachin and at prayer:
And she wudna be in want o't
Awa up there.

Day is Düne

Lully, lully, my ain wee dearie:
Lully, lully, my ain wee doo:
Sae far awa and peerieweerie
Is the hurlie o' the world noo.

And a' the noddin pows are weary;
And a' the fitterin feet come in:
Lully, lully, my ain wee dearie,
The darg is owre and the day is düne.

---

streekit: laid out; **kist**: coffin, chest; **pows**: heads;
peerie-weerie: very small

Ae Nicht at Amulree

Whan Little Dunnin' was a spree,
And no a name as noo,
Wull Todd wha wrocht at Amulree
Gaed hame byordinar fou.

The hairst had a' been gether'd in:
The nicht was snell but clear:
And owre the cantle o' the müne
God keekit here and there.

Whan God saw Wull he gien a lauch
And drappit lichtly doun;
Syne stüde ahint a frostit sauch
Or Wull cam styterin on.

Straucht oot He breeng'd, and blared: 'Wull Todd!'
Blythe as Saint Johnstoun's bell:
'My God!' gowp'd Wull: 'Ye'r richt,' says God:
'I'm gled to meet yersel.'

---

spree: joke; **cantle**: ridge; **sauch**: willow

Empery

Alexander was greetin
Ahint the tent's flap-door:
'Heh!' speer'd the keekin trollop:
'What are ye greetin for?'

'Am I no Alexander
Wi' the hale world on my back?
But noo that I've taen the world
There's naething mair to tak.'

'Blubber awa!' yapp't the baggage:
'Gin it does ye onie guid:
I thocht ye were maybe minded
O' the braw lads that are dead.'

The Princess Anastasia

The Princess Anastasia
Look't frae the turret wa';
And saw ahint the mirkl'd hill
A flichterin star fa'.

The Princess Anastasia
Stüde in the licht o' the müne,
And ane be ane her siller tears
Drapp't clear and glisterin.

The Whup

Within the pooer o' His grup
God's forkit levin, like a whup,
Streeks a' aroun':
And blinds the e'en, and wi' a crack
Richt on Ben Vrackie's muckle back
Comes dingin doun.

The Bairn

The winter's awa; and yonder's the spring
Comin' owre the green braes:
And I canna but greet, while a' the birds sing,
I canna but greet;
For it micht hae been you, wi' your sma', lauchin' face,
Comin' in frae the weet.

---

whup: an instant

The Hurdy-Gurdy Man

The hurdy-gurdy man gangs by
And dings a sang on the stany air;
The weather-cocks begin to craw,
Flap their feathers, and flee awa;
Houses fa' sindry wi' the soun'
The hale o' the city is murlin' doun.
Come out! Come out! wha wudna steer
(Nane but the deid cud bide alane)
The habbie-horses reenge in a ring
Birlin' roun' wi' a wudden fling
Whaur the grass fleurs frae the causey-stane:
And cantl'd asclent the blue o' space,
Far abüne a' the soundin' fair,
A swing gaes up into the licht
And I see your face wi' yon look, aye there,
That swither'd atween joy and fricht.

---

sindry: in pieces; **murlin'**: crumbling; **steer**: move

Ca' Awa

O! gin a penny in the slot
Gar'd the hale o' the planets choir,
We wud be haudin the world thegither
Wi' orra bits o' wire.

And gin a penny in the slot
Brocht the bricht day up wi' a lowp,
We wud be grammlin owre ane anither
To grab a cannel-dowp.

O! there is gledness in the thocht
That the world has a will o' its ain;
Sae ca' awa through a' kind o' weather
As canty as ye can.

Summer Evening 1942

Above the nightingales which sing
Careless in quiet woods
The noisy birds of iron wing
Into the darkening clouds.

The iron scatters from the sky;
And upon earth the stone:
Kingdoms in their confusion die:
The nightingale sings on.

---

cannel-doup: end of a candle; **canty**: cheerful

In the Fullness of Time

Loosened in quiet from the boughs
The over-ripened fruit drops down;
And the leaf, even when no wind blows.

How silently the year has grown
The ruin of a mighty house:
Bareness of rafter and of stone.

But loud the shouts of broken men,
And dusty tumult, and great woes,
When kingdoms fall that shall not rise again.

June 1943

The simple things which do not pass
Are shining here:
Grass, and the light upon the grass;
Branches which bear
Their glittering leaves of coloured glass.

Steadfast these shine; under clear skies
That look upon
Tyrannic powers which terrorise;
And yet are gone
Like smoke, or mist at the sun-rise.

The Wood

(A Japanese Legend)

A gangrel socht a shady schaw;
And whan he spang'd the syke
He fund a wee bairn sabbin sair
Ahint a divot-dyke.

'Wheesht, wheesht, my dawtie, dinna fret;
What gars ye greet your lane?'
Three times he spak the cannie word
Or she stintit frae her maen

She look't, she laucht, she brocht her hand
Lichltly attour her e'en
And left the bareness o' a broo
Whaur her fleerin face had been.

In fudderin fear the gangrel gaed
Wuldly into the wüd;
Or he cam on a fleury place
Whaur an auld kimmer stüde.

'Puir man, puir man!' the auld wife cried:
'What gars ye gove sae sair?'
'O! I hae seen a weirdly bairn . . . :'
But the gangrel spak nae mair.

---

gangrel; vagrant; **spanged**: cleared; **syke**: small stream;
divot-dyke: a wall of turf; **dawtie**: pet; **stintit**: left;
maen: complaint; **kimmer**: gossip; **gove**: stare wildly

Three times he socht to tell his tale:
Three times nae word was his:
Syne canniely the auld wife speer'd
'Was it oniething like this?'

She look's, she laucht, she brocht her hand
Lichtly attour her e'en;
And left the bareness o' a broo
Whaur her fleerin face had been.

Impromtu Epitaph for Barrie

Here Barrie sleeps: a Peter Pan indeed
Who found but fairies underneath the weed
Which once had been the thistle; and in the knell
Of Albyn heard the echo of a bell
From elfland or the kirk: followed the gleam,
Which had a golden glitter, not upstream
But to the general sea where, with the tide
And the mild winds of sentiment, learned to guide
His craft – with art which cannot be denied.
Thence at rare seasons to his native Thrums
He would return, even as the cuckoo comes,
Only with summer; and, like that lone bird, rest
An egg of wisdom in some broody nest
Of twittering culture. Then to the south
With *Courage!* echoing in the ears of youth:
Courage! – for those who follow and away:
Cuckoo! – for such as, now in winter, stay.

The Shoreless Sea

Above the darkness and earth's wandering hull
A frail moon hovers like a lonely gull.

Autobiography

Out of the darkness of the womb
Into a bed, into a room:
Out of a garden into a town,
And to a country, and up and down
The earth; the touch of women and men
And back into a garden again:
Into a garden; into a room;
Into a bed and into a tomb;
And the darkness of the world's womb.